BARKING MAD
Cautionary Tails!

by
Danae Johnston

The
Book
Castle

First published March 2003
by
The Book Castle
12 Church Street
Dunstable
Bedfordshire
LU5 4RU

ISBN 1 903747 34 1

Typeset and designed by
Priory Graphics,
Flitwick, Bedfordshire
Printed in the United Kingdom
by The Alden Group, Oxford

Contents

Dedication

Thanks to my family who have all had a finger in the pie, especially Sandra, Robert and Rachael, Joanne and James, without whose help there would not have been a book as my computer skills are minimal! Last but not least, David, without whose patience, good humour and help this would never have happened.

Thanks too, to my brother Winston, sister-in-law Elizabeth and Tristan my nephew, for their help and co-operation.

I must also add my gratitude to our friends at Rose-in-Vale and Anne Belam in Devon, who have suffered the antics of the dogs without complaint. In fact, they insist, with pleasure!

Last but not least, my very good friend and veterinary surgeon, Owen, who encouraged us to have a Standard Poodle in the first place and who has looked after us beautifully ever since, although he says ruefully "I did not suggest you had two!"

Danae Johnston
Photo by
Darren Warner@World-Gardens.com

Chapter 1

BUY ONE GET ONE FREE

What possessed us I shall never know, two people on the verge of retirement, happy in our ordered existence; David with his Council work and me with my beloved, and by now, quite famous garden, welcoming visitors to admire the immaculate, weed-free flower beds and green, healthy lawns that were David's special pride. I think our son Robert's persistence in pointing out what a splendid burglar deterrent a dog is, and the ever present threat of a break in, were the deciding factors. So many folk in this area have had unwelcome visitors!

The seed was sown when daughter Robyn and her John, who were temporarily homeless, lived here for ten weeks with their animals, Jason, a huge, long haired, highly intelligent German Shepherd, and Sasha, a German Shepherd collie cross, also long haired, plus three cats. We were so impressed by them, they were so good, that it tipped the balance in favour of adding a canine to our household. Two out of three of our cats had tolerated the invasion well. The visitors were paragons of good behaviour, never a paw was put on the flower beds, barking was reserved for frightening visitors until introductions had been properly made, and incredibly in spite of their size they never seemed to be in the way. We were hooked. It seemed sensible to time the arrival of the future canine for the departure of our visitors; in this way, we reasoned, the cats, whom we adore, would be a bit broken in by the huge doggie presence and would accept a small puppy without too much more trauma.

Having allowed our thoughts to progress this far the big discussion was what variety of dog to choose. Robert's dog is a short-haired German Shepherd who is super with humans but inclined to attack with a view to killing all other male dogs, particularly black ones. I have always loved the appearance of German Shepherds. To me they are beautifully proportioned, a pleasing colour mix and intelligent, but rather a handful for two potential pensioners! My love affair is really with cats - Siamese in particular. They personify grace and rhythm. By comparison most dogs are rough and clumsy, quite lacking in the cats' sinuous charm, but making up for that in bounce and vivacity, depending, of course, on the breed you pick. Then we read an article in Readers Digest about choosing a dog. In the large dog section German Shepherds were dismissed because, due to their great popularity and greedy irresponsible breeding, weak hip joints were all too common. Labradors, also hugely popular, are apparently beginning to show signs of mental instability and have been known to turn on their owners! That was our first two favourites gone. The three big top dogs, according to temperament, health, and intelligence, featured first the Doberman. We did not fancy their docked tails and smallish heads. Second the Staffordshire bull terrier - the writer assured us that they are extremely affectionate, loyal and made excellent pets. David was interested but I was adamant; way back in our youth his cousin had a bull terrier called Jake whose passion in life was to kill cats, encouraged by his heartless owner. As a result I have hated them ever since - they are, to my mind, ugly brutes anyway! The last choice was the Standard Poodle whose virtues were listed as - intelligent, affectionate, very healthy and possessing a coat that does not constantly leave evidence of its presence on every carpet and piece of furniture around. The last asset really appealed to me after our recent invasion. We asked our friend and vet Owen Pinney for his opinion. He was for them and said: 'they are certainly very healthy, we hardly ever see them here and they have lively, attractive personalities.'

That settled it, we started to read the 'ads' in the pet sections of the local papers. Now you must bear in mind that we have only ever had cats. Our experience of dogs was second hand from our children's pets, plus sentimental memories of childhood. In David's home a loveable Airdale bitch called Tess was boss, and in my case a breeding group of Gorden Setters were the pride and joy of my parents in the years leading up to World War Two, when many trophies were borne home in triumph from Crufts. Best of breed, even once best in class. Sadly all that ended when war started and all but two of the dogs were given away to spread the problem of getting enough food for them. Robyn and John had by this time found an old bungalow on an acre of land in the countryside just eight miles away. The land sloped away to a tiny, spring-fed stream; it was quiet, lovely and full of potential. There had originally been a row of four bungalows; two had been modernised and enlarged in a most attractive manner, one was empty and one still had its original owner in residence, a very old gentleman well over ninety. The road was not made up but it was more than compensated for by the wonderful setting. They loved it and, by the time I saw the poodle advertisement, were nearly ready to move. Then I saw the advertisement - Standard Poodles ready now! This meant that if we were serious about becoming dog owners we could get cracking. A phone call was made and an appointment to view arranged!

The place was a shambles, evidence of multiple animal occupancy and hasty clearing up was everywhere. We were shown past boxes in the hall to the front room which was stacked with more travelling boxes, some occupied some not; fish tanks lined the walls and on a small square of carpet in the middle, four fat black curly baby boys were deposited for our inspection. One promptly peed generously. A cloth was quickly produced and the matter shrugged off.

We were not exactly enchanted. They were not as pretty as most puppies and not in the same league for appeal as even the scrawniest kitten. However, we were interested in the adult dog, not the transient, roly-poly puppy! We must have seemed hesitant and, sensing a sale slipping away, the owner spun us a story about an imminent move to some northern destination to start boarding kennels along with the poodle breeding, in view of which she urgently wanted to be rid of the remaining puppies, and we could have one for half price!!! At this point David took total leave of his senses and said: "O.K then, we'll have two!" The owner was delighted and we picked two of the curly puddings. To our intense amusement, she marked them with black felt pens on their pink tummies - the only bit of skin available!

It was arranged that we should pick them up a week later, as we explained our house was somewhat over loaded with animals at that moment and it seemed rather unfair on them to face the trauma of two dogs and six cats, all anti-puppy. Besides which I had mess enough to contend with; the month was December now, and thirty-two paws were always wet and muddy on every re-entry from the garden. To add newspaper and puddles to that was not a situation I wished to embark upon for the sake of a week's delay.

On Tuesday December 16, Robyn, John and their menagerie departed. On Wednesday December 17 at 3 p.m. we rang the bell at the poodle person's residence. On our other visit we had asked to see their mother but we had been told that she was away at present as they had been weaned. It seems incredible now that we were so naive - we could neither of us recall actually seeing a standard poodle in the flesh! At Crufts on TV yes, but it is not the same. We did not know that, even if a fancy trim is not required, they still need cutting at least every six weeks to prevent them becoming matted and unacceptably scruffy. We were going to learn rather quickly! We did innocently remark on our first viewing that they seemed to have huge paws. We were later told that you could guess at a dog's ultimate size by studying its feet.

We had decided on our way to collect them that I would travel in the hatch back section of the Cavalier with them on the way home, as they would be bound to be frightened on their very first car journey and would need mothering. I had a blanket ready and I had put on old jeans and a sweater just in case of an accident! I settled on

4

the hard floor and gathered "the boys" to me. Almost before David moved off, the one I had in my arms peed all over me, and then the other one did likewise. Even now their bodily functions are very often synchronised! After about half a mile had been achieved, the first one was sick. By this time I was sitting in a noxious puddle and bitterly regretting my decision to travel with them. Not to be out-done, number two puked all over my shoe just as we arrived home.

We had prepared a box in the kitchen and newspaper was ready on the floor but the priority was to put them in the sink and rinse them off, followed by a brisk towelling - one each - only then could I shed my disgusting garments and get into the shower.

Anyone who has had a puppy or puppies knows all about the next few weeks. They mostly scored direct hits onto their newspaper. The book said (by now we had several books) not only is it possible to train your dog not to perform in undesirable places, like the pavement, but that with patience and persistence you can get it to do it to command! Well, all I can say is, I have never come across one of these wonderful dogs and, if they do exist, I am sure that they are not poodles!

Our house has an unusual design, because we are on a steep hill with a superb view at the back. The kitchen is next to the front door and there is no "back" door as such; you have to go out of the front door, turn left, down the steps, through the gate to the back of the house to get to the utility room which is at garden level. It is here with the boiler and the washing machine that the cats rule. They have their basket on top of the boiler and they spend most of their time snoozing in the lovely warmth, peaceful, curled up together like pieces of a jigsaw. The cat flap provides exit and entrance to the garden at their pleasure, and all is well in their heaven. Correction - it used to be. In an attempt to hurry the "getting to know you" stage, we shut the boys in with them for a while everyday. The girls were FURIOUS; they rebuffed the puppies' enthusiastic efforts to jump up to them with blood-curdling oaths which baffled them. Then they played among themselves on the floor thereby preventing the cats from wandering out via the flap for a stroll, a spot of frog stalking or bird-watching should it take their fancy. Instead they fixed the enemy with three pairs of hostile, ice-blue eyes, and any leap that came within range of their lightning paws got a bunch of fives and a bloody nose! Which did nothing to improve relations.

When they were not eating or sleeping, the puppies played at shredding their bed, a replaceable cardboard box, or pulling their blanket around, tumbling and chasing until they were exhausted and ready to sleep again. I had to leave them to their own devices each morning while I went about the town visiting my chiropody patients. Their antics and misdemeanours made a pleasant change of topic from the weather (isn't it cold - isn't it hot - isn't it windy - isn't it wet etc.) or their aches and pains. Really doggy patients were fascinated and enjoyed reliving their own experiences. Without exception the serious dog owners said in disbelief: "you've got two boys?"

I explained dozens of times that a girl had been our intended choice but there were none, and in view of our daily absence we thought two would be company for each other. Heads were shaken, desperate problems were forecast when they grew up. We both replied that the die was cast and we would tackle the problems as they arose - if they arose.

When Robert heard that we had not only got two dogs, not a bitch and that they were both as black as the ace of spades, he was convinced that Max would annihilate them. Robyn was unhappy about Jason's reaction too, he has always been top dog and there is no love lost between him and other dogs either. They both decided that the best way forward would be to introduce them all as soon as they had had their vaccinations and from then on have lots of contact with each other and hope for the best. In our status of novice dog owners already showing signs of irresponsibility, we agreed with everything.

The six weeks to vaccination went very fast; they were growing at a huge rate on a diet of raw tripe (ugh) plus weetabix and egg for

Getting to know you

breakfast and milk and biscuits at bedtime. Our doggy training manuals were diligently read and we made valiant attempts to follow the instructions. Toilet training was a high priority, but due to the strange geography of the house it was not possible to just open the back door and let them wander in and out in the hope that they would get the message. We tried it in the utility room but the cats made such a fuss about feeling cold - it was mid-winter - that we meekly continued to put newspaper down in the kitchen, and told each other they were still only babies.

Remembering their first car ride, I decided to take them for their jabs each in one of the cats' travel baskets suitably lined with newspaper. It was just as well; when I lifted them out for inspection they were in an indescribable mess, soaked in wee and car sick too. Owen is getting immune to such situations and has a great sense of humour. He contented himself with saying he was glad they were not his and we were gluttons for punishment taking on two. He had only suggested that we had one! The jabs were administered with great speed and expertise and the revolting objects returned to the basket at arm's length. His nurse meanwhile had replaced the newspaper for us.

Now they were free to mingle. Jason and Sasha were already invited to come walking next day. The introductions were made, everyone was on best behaviour, the puppies rolled on their backs and presented their fat tummies for a thorough inspection. Jason passed them without enthusiasm but without aggression either. They seemed to know he was boss and no nonsense would be tolerated. Apparently - the book says - puppies have a particular scent which identifies them to adult dogs and keeps them safe from harm - thank goodness for that!

They knew their names by now of course, and we could usually tell them apart, but we made it easier by giving them a different collar. Tom had a red collar and Gill a blue one. David and I had almost come to blows over their names. I thought Bill and Ben would be highly appropriate but he hated that, Sooty and Sweep - too childish. Someone mischievously suggested Rasta and Farian, with their black curls in mind! I imagined us shouting across the park - not likely! Tom-Gill is a tiny but fascinating stream tucked away near Tarn Howes in our beloved Cumbria. We love the Lake District and return several times a year; at that stage in our innocence we even imagined taking them with us in years to come, but more of that anon.

They were growing so fast that we needed to leave them in the garden on their own for a good run every day; dog proof garden fences became a priority. The top garden was fairly secure but that was the older section and full of herbaceous treasures. The lower part was less densely planted, with the emphasis on trees and shrubs. That was the obvious part to choose, but the fence was just post and wire with an embryo holly hedge started with seedlings round two sides, and on the other side of the fence is a wood, a fascinating wood full of strange smells like deer and squirrel. Beyond that lies a very busy main road, so the wood would be forever out of bounds.

Fences are very expensive and we needed about eighty metres. The best option seemed to be chestnut paling and, although it is not very attractive, we thought the holly would soon hide it, so we went ahead and it was soon in place with the help of a friend. We had not chosen very well. The stakes that make up the fence are each separated from the next by a strong twist of wire and are split not sawn. Although fairly straight, the occasional one has a distinct curve and Murphy's law dictates that, should a particular stake curve to the right, its neighbour will also be a curved one and will be fixed in the opposite direction. At a glance the dogs looked far too fat to squeeze through, but it took them no time at all to find the largest gaps...

We are enthusiastic wildlife fans and encourage a wide range of feathered and furry beasties into the garden by growing plants with tasty berries for the birds and flowers brimming with nectar for the butterflies. Sadly, pretty as they are, the muntjac deer, which live in the wood, kill trees and shrubs by stripping the bark as well as eating a wide range of plants, so they are not welcome. All my trees have to have guards round them, which does not improve their appearance. We hoped that a side benefit of the fence would be to keep them out, but no such luck. They, too, quickly found those places in the fence.

Imagine my horror when, early one morning after I had made the tea, I went to let them in from their first quick run, and they had vanished. They had to be in the wood. Our panic was rising as we visualised the already busy road. David did not stop to dress, he went after them in pyjamas, dressing gown and wellies, while I called and coaxed from the right side of the fence. We soon located them crashing about like hippos in this wonderful, new, exciting place but they were having a ball, and there was no way they were coming yet. David was cursing as the thick hawthorn bushes clawed at him, and I was glad I had not followed him in my long nightie and garden anorak. Thank goodness, although the neighbours could have heard us, there was no way they could see us. Eventually, David captured one and passed it over to me, and the other then gave up without more protest and returned under David's arm like a parcel. That cuppa, when we finally drank it, was heavenly. The puppies, oblivious of the panic they had caused, snored gently in their box, dreaming of BIG GAME no doubt!

As a result of this little escapade we went shopping again and bought rolls of cattle wire, the rectangular stuff that farmers use miles of. We nailed this onto the fence. A painful exercise; the wire was tightly rolled and no warning note said "Danger! Release and stand back". We cut the holding wire, and the thing came alive, unrolling within itself like a ringlet when the curler is removed, only really viciously. When it stopped its little game, we approached cautiously and lifted it to the fence, hammer and staples at the ready. It is not easy to hammer staples in straight, even if everything is keeping still and the staple is at the right angle. When you are fighting to unroll the now reluctant wire and attach it, while crouched in a very

It took us no time to find the largest gaps in the fence.

narrow space with a holly bush attacking from behind, it is a nightmare. The staples pinged off time after time until the air and fingers were blue. The wretched stuff was now determined not to be unrolled and curled tenaciously round each holly bush in turn as we pushed our painful way along. Why on earth we did not use chicken wire I cannot imagine, it would have been so much easier to handle. At any rate we comforted ourselves that nothing bigger than a mouse would get through now and the deer would have to look for new mischief. The boys, when released into the garden again, spent ages inspecting every inch of the fence looking for a gap, but were forced to concede defeat.

The next necessity was to teach them to walk on a lead. This we did in the garden, with much hilarity as they played cats cradle round each other and us. It would have been more intelligent to have one dog each, but I insisted David had both so that I could take pictures!

At this time we had a lady coming to our chiropody practice for treatment who ran a "poodle parlour". She was David's patient and he wasted no time in picking her brains about poodles in general, and cutting them in particular. The cost of a professional barbering job was around twenty-five pounds per dog, something else we had overlooked when we chose the breed! It seems so obvious now, but we had simply not thought further than that they did not shed any hair. What greenhorns we were!

Barbara was our friend's name and, when she confided in us that her back was giving her problems and she was thinking of giving up grooming really big dogs, we did not feel we were taking the bread from her mouth by doing a D.I.Y job on the boys. She was absolutely super. Not only did she tell us what equipment we would need and where to get it, she also invited me to watch her at work. I stood in on a session with a big poodle like ours and even had a go with the clipper. Fortunately they, as a breed, love attention of any kind and that includes being clipped; only their feet and faces are difficult - as for the rest, if they were cats they would purr!

Photo call.

13

We had a round trip of over a hundred miles to find the stockist of the special Oster clipper plus scissors and shampoo; it was incredible to see the doggy cosmetics that were available. We had tentatively asked Barbara if the electric clippers sold for humans would be any good and had been told in no uncertain terms that they would not last five minutes, and anyway the £150 that the Oster cost would soon be made up if we were paying £50 (£25 each) every six weeks for a pukka job.

Bursting with confidence we could not wait to get home and "have a go". Much debate went on as to where, and on what table, the deed should be done. The kitchen table seemed the obvious choice and we pushed it up to the cupboard to prevent escapes or unscheduled dismounting from one side at least. Our youngest daughter Jo's boyfriend helped, trying to hold a squirming dog while David started the clipper and had first go. It was Gill and he hated it, probably the forcible restraint as much as the vibrating sensation and noise. David only had a few hicuppy runs down his back before we abandoned it in favour of scissors. Tom was just as awkward and all we succeeded in doing was making an incredible mess on the floor with their wool. I had, as usual indoors, only got socks on, and they had acquired thick black soles to them; we swept up three-quarters of a carrier bag of wool and discovered that an airborne mist of fine hair had settled on every surface in the kitchen. It took ages to wipe it all down and we were finding black hair in our food for days afterwards. It had not been a good choice.

Now that they were able to go out into the big world, we took them walking everyday. About once a week, Robyn would bring Jason and Sasha and we would go together. They all squeezed into her Nova, causing quite a stir at corners and traffic lights when excited barking drew heads towards the steamy windows and solid mass of seething dog. You could see people trying to count how many there were and pointing them out to their offspring. Not that anyone was allowed to miss seeing us, Jason and Sasha made sure of that. They deafened us.

The basic idea, apart from enjoying each other's company, was that the boys would learn by example how to behave - what a joke! Our favourite walk was through farm land, very quiet and hazard free with ample bridleways and generous hedges. While Robyn's pair kept on the paths within a few yards of us, my two showed no fear of getting lost or being far away. The moment their leads were released they just took off like arrows across the fields, raising flocks of gulls and speeding away until they were just black specks. They always came back eventually and I stopped panicking after a bit, but nothing would stop this behaviour; some madness seemed to seize them. We tried everything in the book, and all Robyn's experience had taught her, but it was no use.

We smacked them when they did eventually come back; all that did was to make them keep a safe distance from us and not be caught. We tried coaxing and rewarding them with a biscuit when they did return. Yes, the biscuits were nice, but the thrill of the chase was better. Not only did they chase seagulls, they chased everything that moved; horses - very embarrassing; trailers and tractors - very worrying; pheasants - unpopular with the farmer; other dogs and small people on bicycles with fluorescent head gear - who usually fell off. We spent our time shouting apologies and trying to excuse them with "they are only babies!" A likely story, they were growing so fast they seemed nearly as big as Sasha and they were not yet six months old! If we saw the hazard in time we would grab them and put leads on, but only too often they saw the game first and were away.

Most people were very forgiving when they learned their age and they did look very cute and different with our DIY haircuts. Other dog owners were intrigued to know what breed they were, and they got away with their misdemeanours. We never did find out what happened on one occasion when they spied horse riders turning onto our track some hundred yards ahead and away from us over a slight rise and out of sight. The boys shot after them like black missiles, totally deaf to our cries and they too disappeared over the hill and were gone about five minutes, while we imagined novice riders falling off, horses bolting, total chaos - we never knew. They came galloping back out of the west like two cowboys, side by side, tongues hanging out, ears flapping and big grins on their faces. We pretended they were not our dogs (we often found ourselves doing that!)

When another four weeks had elapsed we began to panic about cutting them again; they were so shaggy already, two more weeks was going to make it very hard work. We debated and argued. If not in the kitchen where can we do the deed? It is essential in order to get through their wool that they start with a shampoo - a rather wet business for all of us! We waited for a warmish day and bathed them outside in an old baby bath. We all got soaked as expected. They did not think much of the performance and they not only shook and wriggled while in the water, they also waited till they were back indoors and shook and shook, spraying the walls, washing machine and boiler, before we had a chance to towel them. We had put a small, sturdy table in the utility room to cut them on and by shutting one out we made much better progress with the cutter. It was only legs, feet and faces that had to be scissored this time. My regular grooming sessions had accustomed them to the handling and most of the time they enjoyed it. If they were both in the room together they would vie with each other for next turn.

This system only worked twice - by Easter they had outgrown the table and we had to think again.

They soon grew enough to reach the work tops and cat food!

Chapter 2

CANINE CAPERS

In order to drum some pavement manners into them, at least twice a week I took them to the park ten minutes walk away. I always used the same route, avoiding the main road for fear they saw a dog or cat on the other side and dived over to say hello. I have become a familiar sight, whizzing along at scout's pace behind two excited black delinquents. Cheery greetings of "Taking you for a walk are they?" float after me as I shoot past. When they snapped their leather leads we introduced them to choke chains and chain leads with a leather handle that would stand the strain. In order for a choke chain to be effective it has to be slack, then the theory is that you give it a sharp jerk, which tightens it round the throat, at the same time saying 'heel, heel'. The dog obediently stops pulling and walks quietly beside you - rubbish! From the moment I shut the front door behind me I am whisked along, chains tight, leads straining and no hope of catching up enough for them to slacken off, and certainly no breath to shout 'heel' or anything else!

Sometimes for a change they would take opposite sides round a lamppost and bring me to an undignified halt with one arm round each side. Another trick was for one to stop dead to investigate a delicious smell while the other forged ahead regardless, leaving me stretched painfully in the middle. The main road had to be crossed somewhere and, as there is a convenient zebra crossing, we use it. I try to make this another lesson (like not pulling - ha ha). I have a mental picture of two gorgeous Labradors I have seen on their walk while I am waiting at the lights in the car, and whose bottoms hit the pavement instantly on the command "sit" and then wait quietly for the word "cross" before they move an inch. My ambition is to achieve this miracle too. Our performance is rather different. At home they will "sit" for a biscuit every time, but on the edge of the pavement

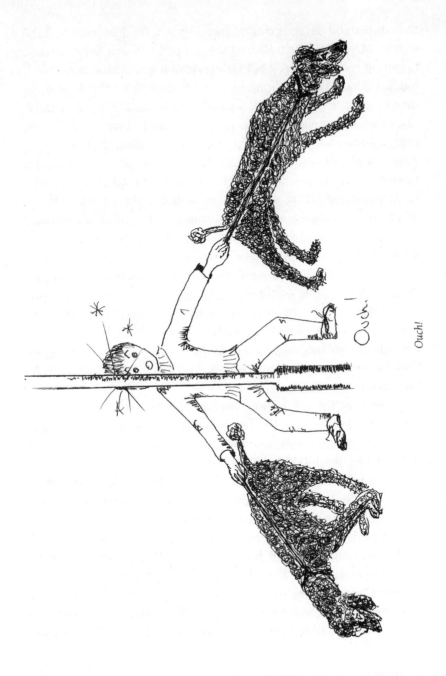

Ouch!

they dither and delay, because I haven't got a third hand to find the biscuit. Meanwhile the traffic, which stopped ages ago to let us cross, is getting restless, so we abandon the lesson and scuttle across with much embarrassed head nodding and mouthing "thank you" to drivers. I cannot wave thank you because my hands are very busy! The other scenario is for us to lurk near by until there is a lull in the traffic, then dash to the crossing and go through the lesson; sometimes we succeed but it is such a busy road that usually we are beaten before we get 'sat' by not one car but a queue of assorted vehicles waiting for us, and again we abandon the attempt. On the other side we progress along a moderately busy road on a bus route.

Our point of crossing here is tricky for a different reason. We must not cross too soon because there are two cats who live on the other side and who are usually relaxing on their driveway. Just past the bus stop on our side lives a vicious dog who snarls and hurls obscenities at them from under its gate, just its snout and teeth visible in the gap - especially its teeth! Both hazards mean active participation by the boys if I dare to actually walk past either; so we carefully cross in between. This time I insist on them sitting on the kerb before we cross, I won't be thwarted again! If the pavement is wet they object and I do not blame them, but rules are rules and I persist until they co-operate. The knot of people at the bus stop enjoy the side show; they watch with great interest - and are quite put out if the bus arrives and they miss the outcome.

On wet, cold days the cat hazard is virtually nil. All felines are in the warm and dry as you would expect of a superior intelligence. Dogs, however, demand their walk whatever the conditions. Other dog walkers en route to and from the park trudge along, heads down collars up, dog noses down too taking in the scent messages from every gate and lamp post, until they meet another dog on a lead that is; then convinced the other dog is about to attack their owner they go bananas, barking, rearing up and lunging towards the threat who is behaving in a similar manner. The pair of them are now so big and strong it takes every ounce of my strength to hang on, and the crazy, infuriating thing is that the dog they are trying to attack is almost certainly one they meet regularly in the park when they are running free, and whom they greet and even have a game with! We dog owners are only too aware that most dogs on a lead are a different animal - rather like some people behind the wheel of a car!

Another situation, less physically demanding of me but highly embarrassing occurs when we pass any dog-less female pedestrian. Gill is the sinner, his nose is at crotch level and the poor woman gets an intimate inspection before I drag him away muttering apologies. Tom meanwhile probably has his nose in her shopping bag in search of biscuits. I try to pass it off with a nonchalant "so sorry, dogs will be dogs, I am afraid they inspect everyone" then I haul them off and hurry away!

Once in the park I thankfully release them and flex my cramped fingers as they shoot away and do two circuits of the park while I stroll along the first section. There are always dogs to greet and pigeons and squirrels to chase. The park is shaped like a rug flopped over a chair, the back and front sections both having playing fields on their lower reaches and thin woodland and rough grass on the steep, high part where we walk. I enjoy a chat along the way with various other regulars. Having a dog is an instant introduction. Dog owners on the whole are a sociable breed and who better to talk "dog" to than another owner? We are constantly asked, "what are they?" Because we do not care for the stylish and to our mind ridiculous coats that their up market relatives sport, ours are barely recognisable as poodles in their "all over the same except where we missed a bit" coats. Judging by the compliments showered on them, most people agree with us.

Most of the time they are not even in sight, dashing to and fro, covering miles in their happy freedom, but they know the routine and come to me at the starting point of the walk and sit like angels to receive a biscuit and have their leads on again; unless a squirrel has just been rash enough to risk a terrestrial dash within their pounce range, which means lots of excited noise and frantic attempts to climb the tree into which the foolhardy beast has just vanished and is at present sitting on a bough well out of range laughing at them. The return trip is much more relaxed. They behave impeccably walking just ahead of me, one on each side and leads slack. I am well aware that this change is entirely due to the fact that they are exhausted, having done about five miles to my one; however, I lavish praise on them in the hope that something will click in their woolly heads and they will always walk that way. Their memories are phenomenal; they only to see a cat once to remember ever after where it was and attempt to check up on it every time we pass. One battle-scarred white tom deliberately taunts them by strolling along the path in full view or just sitting on the pavement, openly daring them to chase him. To be fair to them, chase is all they do, they have never shown any aggression when they have caught up with their target. I would not like to be squirrel at their mercy, however, I think instinct would take over then. I hope I never find out!

The walk home is not often peaceful for long; on one occasion we were stepping it out nicely on the footpath along a short road with a wide grass strip in the centre - a sort of residential dual carriageway - and coming towards us, up the central reservation, was this very small Spaniel and his owner. For some reason they took a particular dislike to this inoffensive little chap and leapt and lunged in full cry. This was too much for him and he turned tail and ran; he ran the same way that we were going and I had to chose rather quickly between letting go or falling flat on my face - I let go. A passing car, seeing a great black dog - Gill - in the middle of the road with his lead trailing, pulled up with a squeal of brakes; this made Gill hesitate for a moment and I managed to put my foot on the lead and recapture him. No so Tom; the Spaniel had disappeared round the corner, with Tom on his heels and his owner a few yards behind Tom. I was miles behind and, by the time I reached the corner, the Spaniel had been rescued and was getting a cuddle and Tom was zigzagging across the road with his lead getting filthy, but too afraid of retribution to come back to me; he was well aware how wicked he had been. I caught up with the perspiring Spaniel owner and explained again that they were only puppies and, apologising profusely, I left with no hard feelings. I did eventually catch the villain and a very chastened dog walked behind me the rest of the way home!

Taking them out, especially on my own, is always an adventure; if all that happens is a few excited exchanges with dogs or cats out of reach in their gardens or behind windows I count myself lucky! One day we had just rounded the corner to the zebra to see a Jack Russell on a lead approaching the crossing from the other way. I tried hard to put on the brakes, but was propelled at high speed to meet it. Its elderly owner was quite oblivious to the imminent, loud encounter. This time the stranger stood his ground and snapped and snarled at them, while they in turn barked furiously and lunged repeatedly at him. I hastily anchored myself by clasping the lollipop pole. They continued to cavort round me like some mad dance routine, shouting insults at the terrier, whose owner, still unaware of my problem, was making tortoise like progress across the road, going our way. What bad luck. I just stayed put, my arms getting stretched like a chimp, and the traffic, thinking I was waiting to cross, stopping and helpfully gesturing me on, enjoying the cabaret, while I in turn tried to indicate with swinging movements of my head that I was not crossing yet, thank you and they should go. My arms of course were fully engaged. Eventually the dogs calmed down and we proceeded, also at a snail's pace, in order not to catch up with the enemy, who to my relief soon turned right, leaving me to go left, and home.

Six months is the acceptable age to begin classes and we wasted no time in enrolling, fondly imagining that, once taught how to behave by an expert, our troubles would be over, what a joke. I am not saying that classes were a complete waste of time and money. They learned to "stay", they could already "sit" - when they chose to, that is - for a biscuit for example. In theory they learned to walk to heel. In class they did it beautifully. They also learned to come instantly if I was holding a smelly piece of liver. What they never mastered was obedience. They were excellent pupils, they did everything required of them, but only when they wanted to and that is how it remained.

The classes were held in a corrugated iron barn with a paved floor. The instructor, a lady, greeted us with "oh, Poodles, both dogs too! You are going to have problems!" We started by sitting on chairs placed at intervals around the wall. She explained that the only way to train a dog is by bribery and that all dogs will sell their souls for liver. She had brought some for us (at twenty pence per bag!). We dutifully equipped ourselves with the messy morsels and returned to our seats. The other puppies and owners studied each other with great interest. There was an exquisite and very superior, mushroom, coloured Great Dane called 'Gucchi' at one end of the hall and at the other an incredibly excited and energetic Yorkie called 'Treacle'. Treacle was the only one who had been to classes before but you would never have guessed! She was bouncy and effervescent, hurling herself from one end of the hut to the other, in and out of the other dogs' legs, back to her mistress and off again all in the wink of an eye while the others just watched, Gucchi in genteel disbelief at such bad manners, Tyson the English Setter and Sheba the German Shepherd watched with envy, wanting to join in. A wonderfully cuddly looking, deep coated, oriental dog, called an Akita, belied his appearance by being very grumpy with everyone, taking every opportunity to nip any one who came in range. We were all sitting with our dogs beside us, apart from Treacle who was everywhere, and one at a time we were instructed to walk round the room and allow our dog to say "hello" to each of the others in turn. David went first with Gill and I followed with Tom. Poodles are extroverts, friendly, interested and pushy, and they were in their element. Once everyone had had a good sniff at everyone else, and the pockets containing liver had been located, we were ready for the serious stuff. Our teacher had brought her own Border Collie just to demonstrate how a dog should behave. She marched up and down with it glued to her left side, its nose an inch from her hand while she did quick turns and reverses without dislodging it. It was then told to 'stay,' which it did of course, never moving a whisker until she gave the command 'come', when it ran and sat in front of her for its piece of liver. We were most impressed, as was intended, and filled with hopeful optimism for the behaviour of our own holy terrors.

Our own demeanour was very important we were told - "you cannot hope to make your dog do what you require if you are not dominant and decisive". She was merciless; one poor man who was hesitant and unsure was told "to pull himself together", how could he expect his animal to obey him if he dithered! This reduced him to an embarrassed and even more dithery state! David was told to "speak up and not mumble!" Then when he lowered his voice several tones and called "Tom-mm-m" she said she did not mean he was to sound like Big Ben!

After a few lessons most pupils were sitting, and staying, and coming, and heeling, and we were kidding ourselves that we were making huge progress. Unfortunately, although ours were usually the first to learn a new command, they flatly refused to go on doing it - 'we got the message' they said, it is boring repeating it! Tom, when told to sit, would promptly lie down and shut his eyes! If you told him to 'lie down' he would only sit, and we should have realised then that we were on to a loser. The instructor appeared to wash her hands of them, referring to them as "the peculiar poodles with the lawn mower cut". This hurt our pride, as we thought we were making quite a good job of their barbering; we did not know then that she owned a doggie shop and poodle parlour! We always arrived early enough to go for a walk on leads around an adjacent sports field to get rid of some of their energy and ensure that they did not pee in the hut as some of the nervous dogs were prone to do, and this worked, so we were spared that embarrassment!

By the time the six weeks were done, ours were 'staying' nearly every time. On the command 'come' they would throw themselves joyfully down the hall, sliding to a halt and knocking us over if we did not dodge in time. Their other trick was to play 'Grandmother's footsteps'- when told to stay, they would sneak a bit nearer each time we turned our backs. Our instructor told us sternly to repeat the exercise until we could do it properly; this caused smug satisfaction to the other owners whose pets had done well, and the unease of those still waiting their turn. She had given up altogether with Treacle, she was unsquashable. On the command 'come' she hurled down the room with huge wheel spin on the concrete and then leapt straight into her owner's arms. By now there were only six of us left, the others had abandoned the classes - in despair presumably. We would occasionally meet one of these stalwarts on the hills with their dogs; to a man they agreed that their dogs were only marginally better-behaved and that as owners we were all failures.

Tom was slightly more obedient than Gill and so at the end of the course, when the decisions had to be made whether to go to stage II or give up, we decided to take Tom only, for a further six weeks, and then practise the lessons at home with Gill too. This was partly because David was finding it very difficult to come due to his Council meetings and I was not allowed to handle two dogs. Also we would save half the cost!

The opening remark of our teacher regarding future "problems" with two male dogs worried us somewhat; as total novices we had not given the matter a second thought when we bought them both. We were told darkly that no responsible breeder would have dreamed of selling two dogs to the same home. We listened to this with dismay, the only advice she could give was for us each to relate to one of them, feeding, grooming, exercising and holding the lead of 'our' dog. If this did not work we could try castration! - poor boys. When we chose them originally, David picked Tom and I picked Gill, so we decided to stick with that. Not so the dogs, Tom decided he was my dog and Gill adopted David so that is the way it has been ever since.

The second course of lessons finished without any noticeable improvement in their behaviour. Indoors, they come immediately because a summons usually means food or a walk. In the garden they avoid the flowerbeds, but it would have been easy to teach them that anyway. Digging is a sin we cannot cure and they vetoed coming to a call or whistle when out walking, because even if a reward was offered it did not make up for being on leads again, they do not normally even raise their heads when we call. Whatever smelly delight they have found is far too interesting.

The period of the next six weeks saw them growing very fast and becoming quite large dogs. Family and friends were always asking how much more they were going to grow and, as we did not like to admit that we did not know, we hedged with replies like "a bit more yet!" or "we shall see" and the doggy experts put on airs and said "They have very big feet, that is a good clue". Oh dear, what had we let ourselves in for!

It must be here - I can smell it.

It was in about mid February when I foolishly left my business appointment diary on the kitchen table. When I found it, it was unrecognisable. The back hard cover was reduced to about one inch wide and the spine had gone at one end. The front cover had lost its corners and had a tasteful embroidery of teeth marks all round the edge. Inside had mainly escaped, apart from having dog-eared and dribbled - on pages. It just was too late to buy another - it would be, wouldn't it! I managed to do a Blue Peter job and concocted a reasonable new cover with cardboard and sticky backed plastic. At least it caused a few laughs from my patients.

My book was not the only casualty; one of the kitchen stools had to have new rungs and a small footstool I use to reach high cupboards had all four corners re-shaped. They had plenty of chewy toys but household items were much more desirable. I bought hide 'bones' and real marrow bones which lasted well past their sell-by dates and became increasingly high, until they had to be relegated to the garden where they were still being enjoyed months later.

Their worst crime was committed one evening when I was out of town at a committee meeting and David was in charge. David is a dormouse. After his evening meal he has to battle to keep his eyes open; not that he usually fights very hard! Even his top favourite TV shows like "Morse" or "Taggart" have gaps in the plot when his eyes refuse to stay open. I try to keep him awake but eventually I give up, and when he wants a re-cap of the last thirty minutes or so I say "oh, get back in your teapot" which goes down rather badly!

On this particular night it was very late; my meeting had gone on till nearly 11.00 p.m. and on reaching the motorway junction I had used to get there it was to find a "Closed Northbound" notice. My heart sank. I had no map, the district was totally strange to me and, inevitably in the maze of suburban streets, I got lost. There are never any sign posts when you need them, are there? When I finally reached home, it was around midnight and David was in the kitchen, obviously looking out for me. I put his concern down to the lateness of the hour and my safety, but after I had explained about my problems it was obvious he had something on his mind. He said the dogs had had a go at my mat - what he meant was that my precious 5ft x 3ft hearth rug, lovingly made over a period of a year, was now ruined. I was very proud of this rug; not only had I laboriously made it by hooking the wool onto a canvas backing, I had also designed it especially for the lounge. He had obviously been sound asleep when the villains had started to fight over it, with the result that 9" of one end was gone and odd snags and holes decorated the rest.

I was really upset; it looked irreparable, and I went to bed not speaking to him and thoroughly miserable. Next day after work I really examined it. David had picked up the wool that they hadn't actually eaten and put it in a bag - whether to hide the evidence or preserve something for repairs I don't know. It had a wide cream edge and the main pattern was still intact. I could not just tidy the damaged edge as it would have looked very odd. I decided to shorten the other end a little which got rid of a damaged corner, and with the wool and the bits he had picked up I grafted on a piece more canvas and re-made the bad end. From the top it looks O.K. but underneath it tells a story. It took me a day or two to forgive David and the dogs, and the house was heavy with "atmosphere" until I did!

Chapter 3

RUB-A-DUB-DUB

The bath time problem was still with us at Easter when they were six months old. We remembered an old cast iron Victorian bath, a relic from a re-vamp of the old bathroom at our business premises. The plumber had wanted to smash it up at the time but I had insisted it came home and we buried it to use as a wild-life pool. Here lay the answer. I emptied it and excavated the earth from round it, then enlisted Robert and James help to get it out and carry it (it weighed a ton) to the back of the house under the balcony, only a few feet from the door into the utility room and a water supply. Its claw feet had rusted away but I made it steady on bricks and painted it black. It looked awful but it was just perfect for the job, being deeper and narrower than modern baths. We could use a hose to fill it and just pull the plug to let it drain into the garden afterwards. The appearance of the bath was worrying - our summer garden visitors would not be impressed! However, I built an ornamental wall as close as possible round it, using small pieces of broken paving, and finished just under the lip. We then added a marine ply lid that was also very useful as a table top for refreshments on charity days. I just thank goodness that I insisted they did not smash it up, although because of its weight I was very unpopular at the time!

It started on Thursday night. Gill was obviously loose and desperate and he made a mess on the vinyl downstairs. I cleaned it up and did not scold him. He seemed fine in himself and normal in that department on Friday so we forgot it, but Saturday was the sort of day you wish you had stayed in bed all day. He had had really bad diarrhoea in the night in the main hall where they sleep. It was all over his blanket, all over the carpet and he had also used his tail as a paint brush to decorate the chair seats - they were just the right height!!! The doors and walls had also not missed out. What a sight and smell to greet you on an empty stomach! It was no joke. I donned rubber gloves and did a preliminary clean up of the house, then sat him on a bucket like a person on the loo and washed his bum and tail. Poor Gill, he felt too bad to even wriggle. David left for work, with relief I suspect!

There is always a Saturday surgery at our vet, so I decided to take him straight down there. He caused a laugh in the waiting room when he decided to sit on my lap - all five stone of him. I was practically invisible under this vast black coward. Owen, remembering their first visit, said "Things don't change much, do they?" and he laughed like mad when I described the redecorating of the hall in poo-brown. He prescribed a huge tub of pills, a kaolin and antibiotic mix, four to be taken at once, thereafter twice a day. We gave Gill the first dose as soon as we got back. I was just in time to make my weekly phone call to my mother. I told her the story, expecting sympathy, but she just capped my account with her own doggy horror stories of long ago.

To add to the trauma, the next day, Sunday, I was entertaining to lunch four relative strangers, my son's best friend, his sister and parents. The two boys were planning a world tour backpacking and this was an ideal way to all get together and chat it over. My carefully arranged timetable of cooking and making the house spick and span had gone out of the window. Instead I spent the morning washing walls and carpets before trying to sterilise my own person and the kitchen, and then making a quick sausage toad for lunch. I managed to get everything fairly ship shape and, by the time David came home, what I needed was a large dose of sympathy, what he wanted was his lunch!

After lunch he took them both out to help him cut the grass. Did he sense my need to be shot of them for a while? Gill appeared to be totally recovered and they romped around as usual. I vacuumed and dusted all afternoon, until by 4.55 p.m. I had all the places that the visitors were likely to go, sweet and sparkling at last, and I flopped on the bed exhausted, only to be joined by all three cats who were delighted to get me on my own and lost no time in arranging themselves on various soft bits of my anatomy. For twenty minutes none of us moved except to breathe, then I heard the mower stop and the sound of it being wheeled back to base, so I knew peace was at an end and a doggy walk would still be expected. I dragged myself back to life and we took them for a short run up at the airport. Back home I did a quick, sinful fry up for supper and collapsed on the sofa, until I could decently go to bed!

Sunday dawned bright and clear. The pills seemed to be working and all was well. The expected visitors are very knowledgeable dog people and Standard Poodles are their special favourites. When James told them initially of our new family they seemed to think it was a huge joke and, when pressed to say why, John would only say "oh, well they have a great sense of humour!" We have found that without OUR sense of humour we should have been tearing our hair on several occasions! They are certainly very comical to watch; they seem to find their legs too long and leave them sticking out at strange angles when they sit. Their necks are also too long and their eyes, rather small for large dogs, are mud-coloured and alert - reminiscent of a chimpanzee. If somebody's nose itches the owner does not just scratch it, oh no, he goes down on his elbows, straightens his back legs, sticks his bum in the air with tail straight up then puts the offending nose itchy side down on the carpet and propels himself along with his back legs, his front legs sliding and his nose getting the blissful friction it needs - an incredible sight! The guests had been well primed on all the dogs' antics by my son and they were looking forward to meeting them, as much as, if not more than, they were looking forward to our company!

I planned to give them a traditional British Sunday roast beef, Yorkshire pudding and roast vegetables followed by apple pie, black currant crumble and cream. There was cheese if anybody could find room. The vegetables turned out perfectly, the beef was tender and even the Yorkshire was good. I glowed with all the compliments and forgot all the hassles of yesterday. We swapped dog stories, laughing at past misdeeds etc. and we soon felt that we had known each other for years.

After coffee it was voted a good idea to get a breath of air and shake lunch down with a wander round the garden. There was a light drizzle falling but no one seemed to mind and the flowers looked lovely, their colours intensified by the wet; the bronze fennel's ferny leaves held millions of droplets, shining like diamonds, and open roses shed photogenic tears in the gentle shower. The dogs came too of course and entertained us by tumbling and chasing like circus clowns. Perhaps they were trying to make up for the last twenty-four hours? The visitors had to travel back to Mansfield, a journey of over a hundred miles so, after we had all had a cuppa, they said good-bye and departed. Although it was only 5.00 p.m. by the time we had washed up and got straight, we were glad to sit down and congratulate ourselves on a very satisfactory day. After all the panic of yesterday it all had gone like clockwork.

Next morning, Monday, between David making the tea and us getting dressed, someone helped themselves to the pot of kaolin pills, chewed the plastic and sent the pills far and wide on the kitchen floor. I shouted at them both - it made me feel better and then retrieved the pills with a dust pan and brush, blew the fluff off them and put them in a jam jar. The business of administering them is getting easier. At first Gill managed to spit them out time after time; we tried popping a chocolate drop onto the tongue after first pushing the pill as far down the patient's throat as possible. This has been fairly successful. Tom has also been having pills because he showed some symptoms and there was no way I wanted to risk a repeat of Saturday; he takes his like a lamb and waits for the chocolate. Gill tries hard to get the chocolate without taking his pill, but I push it way down his throat and no nonsense. With them both taking pills, we had to return to the surgery for more. I told the tale of the stolen tub and scattered contents and Owen raised his eyes to heaven, seeking help for hopeless owners and wilful dogs. More pills were obtained and eventually both dogs were back to normal - as normal as things ever are since their arrival that is! It would be no exaggeration at all to say that they have changed our lives. They have caused an earthquake in our erstwhile peaceful household.

Our day never now starts with a lie-in; even on Sundays by 7.00 a.m. they are bouncing about with joy at the start of another day and needing to be let out. Having creaked into a vertical posture and staggered to the door, David lets them out through the dining room. They push and shove to be first through the door, then barking furiously they project themselves onto the balcony and down the metal staircase to the garden. The barking plus the clanging of the stairs which ring out with the punishment are the alarm call for the neighbourhood. For ten minutes or so they are shut into the lower garden and David makes tea, brings me a cup in bed and feeds the cats, who, when they hear the dogs' noisy exit, come up via the cat flap and queue at the front door. First thing in the morning is not my best time but David is a wonderfully understanding husband and he knows that that first cuppa is absolutely essential to jump start me. Meanwhile the cats have a peaceful breakfast and, the healing fluid having taken effect, I get up and take over, while David adjourns to the bathroom for the next half hour. As soon as the girls have finished as much as they want, I tip the remainders (why do cats never clear it all in one go?) into one bowl and take it down to the utility room. They troop down after me to resume their sleep in their penthouse on the wardrobe - the boiler is no longer safe. The boys can now reach the basket and although visits to them are in theory always under supervision, in fact I am folding washing or something and they have managed to chew the lower edge of it while I have not been looking and replacement will soon be essential as the side is nearly separated from the base.

The mother cat, Linka, is a wise old bird with fifteen years of experience and two litters of kittens behind her, so she stands no nonsense. Any black nose bouncing above basket level gets a swift right with five hooks. It did not take long or many bloodied noses for their owners to treat the girls with great respect. For weeks when they were puppies we cuddled the cats on our knees in the evenings, while the boys romped around the lounge to accustom them to one another. It was Tabatha the elder daughter who first plucked up courage to come upstairs on her own and find us. She crept tentatively and silently into the lounge the first time, to claim her old position on my knee. When they spotted her and came to investigate, she raised a threatening paw and let fly a few choice adjectives in Siamese and the opposition just melted. She revelled in her superiority and was soon strolling in amongst legs and recumbent bodies without turning a hair. They knew better than to touch her and how she knew it. Linka is more wary and will sidle in when they are not looking and take a devious route behind chairs and the sofa on her way to share my lap. Puska has always been timid. Even before the dogs' arrival, she would run for her life if a visitor came and we fear she will never be really at home with them but we go on carrying her up and cuddling her hoping she will one day come to accept that they will not harm her.

To return to our morning routine - once the cats are in their beds, the dogs are let in again. They have usually put the time to good use, digging enthusiastic holes in the lawn or border, their muddy paws being an immediate give away and, we take them to the scene of the crime and tell them the error of their ways, but we despair of ever stopping this habit, they revel in it. If we are lucky, they will only have been chasing about, following scents left by nocturnal deer (they still get in), rabbits, hedgehogs and the army of squirrels who live in the walnut tree.

To try to stop the damage their digging causes, I went to endless trouble pegging netting to the ground before the plant growth started. I also surrounded the main bed with a palisade of canes pushed into the ground. It was all in vain; they soon found the weak spots and carried on their devastation; as to the lawn, everyday there are new pot-holes. David is in despair. We have tried smacking, scolding and shaking; they cringe away, knowing full well that they have been very naughty but they do it again at the first chance!

They usually flop out somewhere in the way on the floor while I go to and fro preparing breakfast, stepping over the recumbent forms on each trip to the cupboard or fridge. The arrival of the paper boy or postman instantly activates the inert bodies They jump up to look through the kitchen window; with front paws on the work-top, they bark their heads off, competing to see who can be the fiercest. It is absolutely deafening and the object of the uproar is suitably impressed. They have only just started this, previously they rushed to the window but only gazed silently at the intruder. The welcome now given is a splendid warning to any unwanted callers!

They know all the regular visitors and the family, some of whom get a waggy-waggy welcome; Robyn, their favourite, has a really special mugging and it is minutes before she can calm them down enough to speak! My domestic help, who comes once a week, is scared of cats and was not at all sure about the dogs, but having watched them grow from puppies she knows that if she says "sit" very authoritatively, they will, then she gives them a dog biscuit each (supplied by me) and they forget to jump up and all is well. She is now even brave enough to come into the house when I am not there and quite enjoys being able to boss them about.

Good morning, paper boy!

Chapter 4

GO TO JAIL - GO DIRECTLY TO JAIL -
DO NOT PASS "STEPTOES" -
DO NOT COLLECT £200

We knew when we had the dogs that we would not be able to take them with us to our timeshare in the Lakes because of their passion for chasing everything that moves, particularly sheep, but Robyn said she would be pleased to have them while we were away. We were delighted because they adore her and they would love it at "Steptoes", chasing around with Jason and Sasha in their big garden. To get them used to the idea, it was arranged that she should have them for a day while we did major shopping at Milton Keynes. We had not bargained on their incredible jumping ability, and it took Tom about half an hour to get bored and hurdle the fence of about four foot six into next door's chicken run, catch one by the leg and jump back with his prize. Naturally the poor thing objected strongly to this cavalier treatment and made such a racket that Robyn was there to the rescue before any harm was done and almost before he landed on his return trip! The bird appeared unharmed and she popped it back over the fence before giving himself a good ticking off and a thorough shaking, plus a smack or two to really get the message home. He was then shut indoors, in disgrace. It was another reminder, not that we needed one, that they come from jumping stock and it is indelibly printed in their genes. Nothing we have done by way of punishment has had any curbing effect at all. Advice on all sides from owners of Retrievers, Labradors, German Shepherds - and any other breed you can think of, has all been tried and found useless. Standard Poodles are a law unto themselves and the only real sympathy for our problems comes from the rare Standard Poodle owners that we met.

With "Steptoes" out of the running it was now necessary to find kindly comfortable kennels for them. This proved easier than we thought. We discovered that the people from whom we had bought two of our earlier Siamese cats had a breeding and boarding kennel just round the corner from Robyn's new home - we remembered, we had been there thirty years ago to choose the kittens but it was so long ago that we did not associate "Illustria Kennels" with Robyn's new address at the time. It was a very satisfactory if rather expensive answer to the problem. We were glad to know that they were in good hands, well looked after and secure.

Their first visit to "jail" was when they were seven months old. We drove over there very carefully; it was a journey of only eight miles but Tom has continued to be very car sick and we obviously wanted them to make a good impression! At this stage we just put them in the boot of the hatchback with no physical barrier to keep them out of the back seats. We soon had to change that arrangement, as of course the minute we left them they hopped over and sat in the front, only scurrying back when they saw us coming. On this occasion all went well until we were nearly there and then the familiar retching started and Tom put his head on the back of the back seats and puked all over buckles and straps that sprout from the centre of them, neatly filling all the crevices! It was a disgusting task to clean it up, but at least HE was still presentable, thank goodness. The kennel's owner took charge of them and they trotted obediently on their leads, off to their fate without giving us a backward glance. We were relieved but a bit hurt!

Our holiday was splendid. We spent our time walking unless the weather was really bad, and it has to be bad to put us off! But this June was gorgeous and in addition to the magic of mountains and lakes, the meadows were carpeted in wildflowers - ragged robins, sorrel, tall buttercups, polygonum, pink campion and more. The walls are a home to ferns and foxgloves and everywhere are sheep with their new lambs. It is a heaven on earth in June, but no place for dogs, especially ours!

We thought about them a great deal, wondering if they were

miserable and pining. We need not have worried; we were told that they had settled quickly, become instant favourites and been made a great fuss of by all the family. Nevertheless, the greeting we got was wild and overwhelming. They have never been 'licky' dogs. Gill will sniff and nuzzle, and jump up too, if not rebuffed. He might even give you a tiny kiss with the very tip of his tongue if he feels very affectionate. Tom's kiss is an open mouthed engulfing job, done in mid leap. He is brilliant at it and judges the height of his jump perfectly. After not seeing us for a week, it was a different story. Paws were put on shoulders and it was all I could do to keep my feet, so great was their joy at the reunion. We fought them to the car and they jumped in immediately, delighted to be going home. They smelt strongly of disinfectant, but they were in super condition, they had obviously had lots of TLC. They seemed to have grown even bigger! Tom was sick again but we did not care, we were almost as pleased to see them as they were to see us. Once home, they rushed about finding elderly bones, new smells and favourite toys, until eventually they collapsed exhausted and slept like the babies they still really were. For the next few days they did not let me out of their sight, just in case I did another vanishing act.

During their absence the duckweed on the small pool had spread into a solid green mat, so solid that dozey Tom tried to walk on it and fell in. I was gardening and heard the splash. There he was, soaking wet with a fetching new green coat. Unfortunately he shook most of it off before I could get the camera. As is the way with human babies, the older they got the more they developed their individual characters. Tom became more laid back and did not bother if Gill took the lead in everything. He would never stand if he could sit or sit if he could lie down. When travelling in the car it's always Gill who is sitting or standing, watching the traffic, pedestrians and any other dogs who needed warning off with a threatening bark; this would only wake Tom momentarily. In the very early days he hated the car and would tremble violently at the prospect of a ride and had to be lifted in. It was rarely more than a few minutes before he was sick. Presumably it was because it made him feel horrible that he hated it so much, we shall never know. He was nine months old before he was reliably clean and even then he would save the unexpected regurgitation for special occasions when we were dressed up or they were to be shown off to friends, for instance. We are beginning to understand what John meant when he said that they had a sense of humour!

Gill decided early on that he was top dog, and as Tom has gone along with that all has been well, in spite of ominous warnings from well wishers of battles to come, with two male dogs reaching maturity. The dismal prophets foretold green-eyed jealousy for our attention, leading to major fights. We were told of one such foolish person who had taken on two males and now had such problems that they had to be walked separately and could never be left together without a fight developing. The tone of voice used gave us the impression that it was only what we deserved and that doggy relationships would be watched with malicious interest! Three years old was the crunch time when the enmity would reach its peak, apparently. This forecast made us distinctly uneasy and the next time we saw Owen we asked him for advice, thinking he might suggest castration. To our great relief he pooh-poohed the whole idea, saying that if there was going to be trouble it would have happened by now. We make a big effort to be scrupulously fair always, and when doling out tit-bits we always give Gill his treat first in deference to his self-appointed status!

In spite of being top dog at home Gill is a great baby and is in enormous awe of Robert and Max. Neither of them enjoy the relaxed relationship they have with Jason and Sasha. Max always greets them with a little growl to make certain they know he is boss; then they fawn round him, rolling on their backs in total submission and all is well. Robert has tried to teach them some manners from an early age. He disapproves of them anyway (and of us for having them) and speaks with the impressive authority of an 'officer of the law' who expects to be obeyed at once. This reduces Gill to a jelly. Robert only has to come through the door for him to wet himself with anxiety. He puts his head and ears down, and wags his tail, trying his very best to please this super boss-man.

Once after Robert had had cause to scold him for something as we sat round in the lounge, he ran to me, sat all of himself on my lap, and shook. Robert then felt sorry for frightening him and came over to make up, whereupon Gill promptly peed over both of us!! After that Robert tried to soften his manner a little, but Gill remained very much in awe of them both until he was at least nine months old. I love Max and always make a huge fuss of him, and now and then he comes to stay and we dog-sit for a weekend. Walks on these occasions are a different game. Instead of exploding off the instant they are released from their leads, our two cowards walk to heel the whole time, hoping to gain protection from that frightening boss-dog who is nonchalantly trotting to and fro a few yards ahead. This is marvellous for us - we wish we had Max's power. The only trouble being that the walk is exactly that and they return home still full of energy and ready for mischief.

During their first summer I used to shut them onto the balcony while I got on with some task like washing the floor or baking, with which they considered that they should be allowed to help. How we escaped having ghastly tummy upsets I will never know considering the number of times noses and paws would be involved in experimental investigations of cake and pastry mix, but we survived without any problems. They can now reach to the very back of the work-tops and are expert at lifting a dish, especially a forgotten cat bowl, onto the floor and demolishing its contents without spilling a drop or breaking the dish. Cat food and chocolate come equal as the most prized of treats. Using the balcony as a playpen soon had to stop. Once they had conquered their fear of the steep spiral staircase it was no problem to remove the barrier I had put across the top,

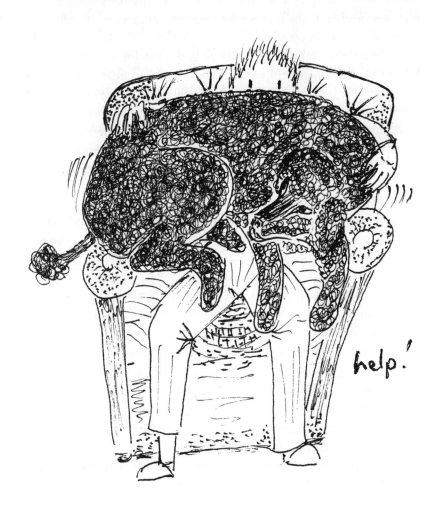

help!

clatter down and bark like lunatics at the cat flap. We could only imagine that they were inviting the cats out to play, but for months and months as soon as they got outside they would dash to the flap and start their racket, shoving their heads through it - all the better to make their presence known. They would give the flap an encouraging jab with a paw to make it swing, then bark even harder, until I was forced to stop whatever I was doing to go and scold them. It was never any use; they resisted for a few minutes and then back they came to start again. Eventually they managed to catch the flap on its outward travel and bite it, leaving a jagged half and a draughty hole. I repaired it by gluing a piece of plywood onto the remnants to make a new flap. This is still functioning but is not very ornamental!

Indoors they go where I go, and if I make the slightest sign that I am about to go downstairs to the utility room where uneaten cat food might be waiting to be nicked, they are there first. The cats used to be fed in the kitchen, but the poor things would starve if they did not get a chance to eat in peace. Puska would get stomach ulcers with the worry of it all. She is a neurotic feline, convinced that the boys would make her their next meal if I was not there to protect her!

Most of their indoor time is spent lying on the carpet in the upper hall on their mats. Soon after we had them we saw an advertisement for pet beds. "Totally indestructible fur rugs, fully washable and guaranteed for the life of the dog". They were expensive but as normal blankets and cushions were often shredded in a day, we decided to invest in the middle size. We bought them one each about the size of a door mat. We simply had no idea that they would get so big. We should have bought hearth rug size! Although they can really only get their head and chests on them, they do indicate where they are to sleep, so they were not wasted. They did tear one, of course, and the firm replaced it by return! I was most impressed. Sadly I have not seen their advertisement again and I fear they were unwise in their replacement promise, and came to grief.

From their sleeping quarters there are three polished wooden stairs down to the main hall which is also polished; then to reach the cats' domain, they have to take a hairpin bend to the left, go down a full flight of carpeted stairs, take another left hand hairpin on vinyl, down three more steep steps and they are there at the door of the utility room. Now imagine me, emerging from the kitchen immediately opposite the stairs. Two heads pop up, they take in the fact that I am carrying cat bowls and they launch themselves onto the polished floor, legs revving furiously and paws sliding on the smooth surface. Then, their momentum recovered, they hurl themselves downstairs, finishing in a heap at the bottom like sacks of coal. They recover again, more wheel spin to get round the corner and there they are pushing and shoving to get through the door first. If I am foolish enough to try to go down at the same time I am flattened against the banisters or swept down at a hair- raising pace with them. The book says "always make your dog wait for you to go through the door". The competition between them to get to the cats first makes them totally deaf to any commands. I prefer to hang back and stay in one piece!

This pantomime is repeated dozens of times a day and the large loose mat that used to be on the floor was whizzed across the hall, at every mad dash, into a favourite small table by the front door, knocking it flying. Fortunately it is a sturdy little thing and has survived; however when I returned from work one day to find the mat chewed up, we abandoned it to the utility room and left the floor bare. The result is that once a week, when my help has polished it, it looks super, the rest of the time, it is decorated with muddy skid marks or just dry dirt according to the weather. I sweep up once a day and do not look at it again. It is too depressing.

It is said that beauty is in the eye of the beholder. At times we think they look beautiful. When they have been newly cut, they undoubtedly look handsome and they win lots of compliments from other dog owners. They look stunning galloping together, flat out, across the playing fields in ever increasing circles, then they slow down to a sort of jog which is very distinctive and apparently peculiar to all poodles. The nearest I can compare it to, is a horse trotting in a dressage exercise, heads up, jaunty and alert, we think this is most attractive - but we are biased! However in repose they are far from elegant. They look as if they have been designed by a committee, long legs, necks which sprout from their shoulders like chimneys, tails which are too short for their necks (not their fault) and, considering how big they are, they have rather small brown eyes. They seem to find it difficult to sit or lie in a tidy comfortable position; often a back leg is left sticking out along the floor ready to trip the unwary while the rest of the dog is sitting or if possible leaning on a convenient wall, chair or human. Sleeping is often done with both front legs stretched to the right and back legs to the left; or on the back, with paws folded each side of the chest and back legs inelegantly splayed - the head and neck is extended, chin skywards and eyes shut. Another strange sleeping posture is on the floor with just their head on a stool or on the sofa. It looks most uncomfortable, but Gill regularly nods off in that position. They are not allowed on the furniture, however Tom has a hilarious habit of backing up to the sofa, and putting his bum down just like a human with all his feet on the floor and his back legs crossed; is so amusing that we let him do it just for laughs. We also let them break the rules for a cuddle now and then. Tabatha regards my lap as her exclusive property and occupies it most of the time, a quick blow to the nose of anyone who disputes this right ensuring she sleeps in peace. If they do catch me ' vacant ' as it were, who can blame them for wanting a share of fuss and affection? The trouble is, it does not stop at a cuddle because the other one is immediately jealous, and starts to aggravate the lap holder, play biting and ear tugging until a pitched battle is taking place, with me helpless underneath the heaving heavyweights. David ignores my cry for help and watches with a grin on his face from the comfort of his armchair. They do not do it to him; I wonder why? These battles are never nasty- in fact as time goes by they get more affectionate towards each other, not less. They will wash each other for ages and then fall asleep with one using the other as a pillow - so much for those pessimistic forecasts!

No walk is without incident, it is always an adventure, anything can happen and does. One day recently, a friend, who works from home and whose door we pass on our way to the park, happened to see us passing by. She dashed to the door and I managed to halt the boys for a moment. This was not easy as we were in overdrive with the park and freedom only a minute away. I managed to have a brief word with her; they gave her the usual comprehensive and embarrassing examination then got bored and strained to get going again, but, before we resumed our headlong race, I promised to come in on the way home for a cuppa and chat. I fervently hoped they would be tired by then and behave themselves. My friend, whose name was Pauline, had no dog at present but had had a lovely Red Setter for many years and was used to, and understanding of, the ways of canines. So I kept my fingers crossed that they would be good and looked forward to our chat. Oh dear, I hoped in vain. We were welcomed in and the first thing Tom did was to cock his leg and pee over an upholstered chair!! I have no idea why he should do such a thing quite out of the blue. I was mortified. Pauline said the garden was fenced, so we shoved them outside, leads still on, and I helped mop up. She was very understanding and kind; she said " think no more of it, and put the kettle on." This done I turned my attention to the garden. I could not immediately see them, so I was instantly anxious. I went out to look properly. They were not in the bushes or behind the hut, they had vanished! An unnoticed hole in the fence had been squeezed through and there they were having a stand-on-our-hind-legs wrestling match on next door's lawn. Just like two kangaroos. Another panic? No, fortunately her neighbour was out and I managed to coax them back before they did any damage to her bushes with their crashing about. They were still trailing their leads and of course by this time they were filthy, mainly with sand. They had gambolled in it, spreading it liberally around until what had been a tidy heap was all over the place with generous amounts on their feet and in their coats. Oh dear!

Their muzzles were covered in it. They had been digging. My poor friend was wonderful; she wiped the leads and I tethered them to the outside of the door so they had no option but to sit or lie and wait for me. I hoped that some of the sand adhering to them would fall off before I had to bring them though the house again. We enjoyed our coffee and actually managed to have a good natter, catching up on each other's news. I said goodbye half an hour or so later and was pressed to pop in again; she sounded as though she really meant it too. What a heroine! I said I would, but privately I thought it would be quite a long time before I did so, in the faint hope that the boys would behave themselves better when they were a bit older. I am still hoping!

Bum on sofa - just like us!

Chapter 5

THEY ARE NOT REAL DOGS,
THEY HAVE BEEN KNITTED

In the first year of their life I was making a fortnightly visit twenty miles away to see a dear old lady, a life long friend of the family now well on into her ninety-fifth year and living in a residential home at Bletchley in Buckinghamshire. When the boys were very young and Tom was so dreadfully car sick, I used to leave them at home, but as he improved we decided it would be good for him to come with me to get him used to longer car journeys in preparation for our holidays and the very long journey to Cornwall in September. They loved the ride as we used a real country route through Woburn deer park and lovely silver birch woodland, carpeted with bracken. We usually saw three or four squirrels crossing and re-crossing the road and they got somewhat excited when they spotted them but soon settled down again. I made sure to give them a run in the park before we arrived, because for the time I was visiting they had to stay in the car, and I hoped they might sleep and not get into any mischief in my absence.

We had been doing this trip for some weeks when one glorious clear blue day the sun was boiling down and there was not a twig of shade anywhere. I felt even with the windows open I could not leave them in the car. I found the matron in her office, explained the problem and asked if I might bring them in. With fingers crossed, I promised they would be good; obviously I would keep their leads on and not let them annoy anyone. She agreed immediately and, after a quick check to make sure the resident cat was not around, I fetched them in.

The dogs love new experiences and were delighted to be introduced to all these nice people sitting round the room making friendly overtures and exclaiming about their size and appearance.

One old dear said they looked like bendy toys, another of the more "with it" ones said "no, black sheep" was what they were. Yet another suggestion was gollywogs but the best description of all was from another friend visiting us at home and seeing them for the first time. He gave a hoot of laughter and said: "They are not real dogs - they have been knitted!" They enjoyed a circuit of the lounge, being petted and patted, before settling on the floor between Edith and myself. She was pleased as Punch at their reception. It was "her" visitor who had provided this welcome diversion and the change of topic from ailments and food. She glowed with importance. Dogs had been a major feature of my young years at a time when Edith was living with us, and our visit sparked reminiscences of those days when my parents' overriding passion was Gordon Setters. The dogs, now completely at home, had sprawled on their sides, legs straight out, eyes shut, do not disturb written all over them. This was fine but we were on the direct route to the loo and at frequent intervals they had to move or be passed with difficulty by with someone with an urgent mission, and a walking frame! They settled back again after each disturbance, but when a huge tea trolley was rolled in there was nowhere their big bodies could be tucked away and I deemed it time to go. Goodbyes were chorused and off we went, for once in their lives they had made a good impression! After that I always took them in with me and the old dears looked forward to seeing them. Sadly our visits came to an end when Edith died just before one Christmas, aged ninety-six.

On these visits David was sometimes able to come too and on these occasions we explored new walking territory. The prettiest way to get from Luton to Bletchley is through the lanes on the edge of the Duke of Bedford's Woburn Estate, as I have described. The woods extend for miles on one side of the road while on the other is the exclusive new golf course where many prestigious competitions are held. It was essential to give this a wide berth; it would never do for one of them to hurdle the fence and join in the game, as they have done on other minor courses we have come across on holiday. We walked purposefully in the other direction with them staying fairly close in the foreign territory, but suddenly they saw a deer, and took off in thrilling chase not to be seen again for ten minutes at least. We did not know the woods and felt quite helpless as usual, so we just stayed put, whistling and shouting; while we waited we remembered how the traffic speeds along the dissecting lanes and prayed silently that they did not get lost or run over. We need not have worried, they came loping back eventually, tongues and ears flopping as usual. We did go back to these same woods several times because they are so beautiful and we enjoyed them so much ourselves, but after they surprised a riding school posse and caused mayhem, with horses rearing, neighing and bolting out of control, all over the place, being terrified by our two idiots barking round their heels, we crossed this walk off our list too. Instead we found a country park on the western side of the Watling Street, near Heath and Reach. At first investigation this seemed a winner. There were fences and no animals other than dogs and humans to worry about. We went there many times during that summer, but of course our dogs could not stay completely out of mischief. Picnickers abounded on warm days and they would go and hang about round a party, looking hungrily at the goodies and making overtures to the participants. These tactics usually produced a tasty reward and so of course the sight of people sitting on the ground with food became a magnet and caused us embarrassment as we extricated them with grovelling apologies.

The parkland has a lake, a deep lake with a small landing stage, which they found very handy to stand on and have a drink. The lake overflows at one end into a boggy area which eventually resolves itself into a small stream. This boggy patch smelt sour without even being disturbed and clouds of gnats danced above the black ooze. The boys, ever curious, decided one day to investigate and had a lovely time squelching about, tummy deep in it. The smell was horrendous, reminiscent of sewers or putrefying remains of heaven knows what.

They looked like chocolate digestive biscuits (as long as you held your breath) and there was no way we could put them in the car in that state, the smell would have been unbearable and the black ooze being spread over the inside of the car was something that I could not bear to think about.... The lake and the landing stage was the answer. We put their leads on and led them, unsuspecting, to the edge. We still held tightly to their leads and pushed them in. It worked splendidly, they hated it of course; it frightened them to be out of their depth and their frantic scrambling to get out washed most of the foul mud off for us. On later visits we kept them on leads as we passed the bog and they voluntarily gave the lake a wide berth!

All our three cats are much older than they look and are pretty healthy but they do get fur-balls from time to time because of their fastidious grooming; they must be spotless, as to dogs - ugh! This licking business not only cleans their coat it also pulls out all the loose hair and because of their rough tongues much of the fur is pulled into their throats and swallowed. This is not usually a problem but if they are moulting or off colour their stomachs revolt and they are either sick or constipated because of it. To solve this problem I keep a tube of cat laxative in the cupboard. It is a meaty flavoured thick gel which you squeeze onto their coat for them to lick off, so much easier than pushing a pill down their throat. Oh foolish me, will I never learn? It did not occur to me that the universal scavengers would find it a delicacy and I left the tube on the kitchen window sill. I am sure you are ahead of me, again, yes they ate it and yes, it had the same effect on dogs as it did on cats. The morning after found me in my nightie, rubber gloves and wellies clearing up the vinyl in the lower hall. David's "you should just see what you look like!" failed to raise a smile, my sense of humour had temporarily deserted me!

It is unusual, thank goodness, to have this kind of unpleasant surprise waiting for me in the morning but one March, when they were five months old, we had an overnight guest. A Very Important Person, the national chairman of my horticultural society no less! She was to give our local branch a talk on the Monday evening and was travelling to London next day for a council meeting. I met her train and brought her home for a meal, a chat and of course a look at the garden before we went to the meeting. It was a good evening, she is a humorous speaker and everyone enjoyed themselves, then I took her home, settled her in my guest room and bade her 'good night!'

She was alone on the lower ground floor as our bedroom and bathroom are on the first floor. To get to the main bathroom she had to cross the vinyl floor... We woke next morning to a familiar smell - I said a silent prayer "oh no, please, not that." But it was; two piles! Once again it was me who cleared up while David made tea. We were both fervently hoping that our guest had not made a nocturnal trip to the bathroom! I took her morning tea in to her and enquired whether she had slept well. She assured me she had and I dared to hope that she was not aware of the dogs' faux-pas. Once breakfast was over, I could contain myself no longer and I asked her if she had needed to get out of bed in the night. She roared with laughter and said she had, and that she was very glad she had put the hall light on!! I was most embarrassed but she was splendid and made a joke of it. She promised not to tell a soul. She is very fond of animals and knows just how they can let you down. We parted even better friends because of it, which just shows what a sport she is!

The training classes are behind us and in some ways the dogs are settling down to being responsible boys. They still refuse to come to a call when out walking, neither can they control their excitement enough to 'heel' when starting out for a walk from home. On the way home, however, they can behave beautifully, which proves that they know what to do but choose not to do it!

Their major sin in my eyes, and one that gets worse rather than better, is their compulsion to dig. I have many unusual and interesting plants which I have collected over many years and consequently the first thing I taught them was "off the garden!" I shouted this command the instant a paw strayed from the lawn or path. They picked it up very quickly and I was delighted with them, but then one day after they had been on their own in the lower garden, I found a newly planted shrub lying broken and dried up on the lawn and a hole where it had been, much enlarged. So great had been their enthusiasm for their task that the earth was scattered yards away. I was furious with them but also puzzled by this sudden change in behaviour. I took them to the scene of the crime, scolded and shook them, then I replanted the battered victim without much hope for its survival. It died of course.

I soon solved the riddle, I had used bone meal in the hole, I always do, and their sensitive hooters had smelt it in spite of it being buried. They must have been puzzled to smell a lovely bone and yet not be able to find one!

A helpful friend suggested that we buried two or three tasty bones somewhere that did not matter if they dug, it would direct their new hobby into the harmless area. Part of the lower garden is an embryo spinney planted with, as yet, small trees and carpeted with snowdrops and bluebells as well as an increasing number of primroses and foxgloves in their season. They are the welcome plants, but there are also nettles galore and lots of cow parsley so a few 'digs' could be tolerated. The trees all have guards to protect their bark from the muntjac deer; we added large flint stones and logs around their roots and then duly buried the bones well away from them. It was a total waste of time, as they dug everywhere but there! The lawn has shallow scrapes all over the place, while on the beds their excavations in the soft ground were impressive, needing in some cases several buckets of earth to repair. The original soil was spread too thinly over a large area to retrieve!

They know they have been naughty and when we discover a new hole, we grab them and haul them to the scene of the crime, while they try to go into reverse gear and apply the bakes in an effort to avoid our wrath. We have smacked, we have scolded, and we have shaken them, all to no avail.

I think they are frustrated truffle hounds.

In order to try and protect my beloved borders during the winter I even pegged clematis netting down onto the soil and just cut it a little for the larger plants, I hoped that it would be 'invisible' and everything would grow though it. It worked fairly well, but weeding and new planting was terribly difficult and they still manage to scrabble round the edges, but never when I am looking; they are far too canny to be caught in the act! I am in despair. I wonder how much electric cattle fencing costs? They would probably jump over that! Their huge feet do so much damage in seconds by exposing roots and burying surrounding plants with the spoil. It makes me feel murderous when I discover a new hole in spite of all my efforts to prevent them doing it.

Apart from digging, their play chasing produces great scrapes in the grass and, although most of the time they go around the planted parts, the sight of a squirrel or a cat and the rules are forgotten as they pelt in pursuit. I am not cross with them for that, after all they are only dogs, but I draw the line at them rushing to the fence and standing on the border to bark furiously every time my neighbours come out into their garden. They do not harm the soft fruit bushes but it is embarrassing to have to constantly apologise for their noise.

We hit on a novel way of protecting the lawn in winter when the surface is very soft and vulnerable. We have around twelve discarded milk crates that are used to support table tops (old doors) for plant sales in the summer. We arrange a slalom course along their favourite route and change it all the time to spread the wear. It does have the effect of making the garden look like Steptoes' yard, especially as we have added other junky objects as we have needed to; we just have to stall any unexpected visitors until we have had a clear up and chucked the rubbish behind the shed!

The winter slalom course.

Chapter 6

WALKING IN THE GIANTS' FOOTSTEPS

We live in the chalky embrace of the Chiltern Hills. Dunstable Downs, Whipsnade Wild Animal Park and Ivinghoe Beacon lie over to the west of us, Sundon country park is further north from Luton, and Sharpenhoe Clappers and Pegsdon hills continue the arc eastwards. All these areas are renowned beauty spots and are owned variously by the National Trust, the local authority and local Wildlife Trust. They are veined with footpaths and make dog walking an even greater pleasure. We have been re-discovering the favourite haunts of our childhood when we spent long summer holidays cycling up and down these hills. Cheese and tomato sandwiches, tizer and apples were stowed in our saddle bags to sustain us until tea time - happy days.

Latterly we have preferred to stay in the garden and avoid the traffic jams that fine weekends bring, feeling very smug as we relax on our loungers and listen to the traffic on the main road. However our choice now is simple: either we take these energetic monsters out for a good run or they go cracker-dog and wreck the garden.

Dunstable Downs is the best choice for a fine windy weekday; with good visibility you can look out over three counties or watch the gliders being hauled up to ride the thermals above you. If it is too popular at weekends, then Sundon Park is a better bet. Here there is a varied mix of undulating fields and mixed woodland which is slashed by precipitous chalk gullies gouged out by glaciers in the ice age. There are hundreds of rabbits in the hills, and plenty of other dogs to greet; our dogs love it. It is especially beautiful in the spring when dog violets carpet the ground. If we were really energetic we could walk eastwards across Sundon hills and woods and cross the lane to the Clappers, another wonderful area which culminates in a dramatic hill crowned with massive old beech trees which seem to rise suddenly from the fields and are visible for miles.

When I was a child my father told me the story of its origin. Apparently there was a giant who lived in Barton village way down at the foot of the hills and he had a violent quarrel with another giant who lived in Luton six miles away. The Barton giant decided to finish the Luton giant once and for all, so he filled a wheel barrow with earth and started to push it up the long hill, intending to bury his enemy's house. He was nearly at the top and feeling very hot and tired when he met a man with a sack on his back coming the other way. He greeted him and asked if he was going the right way to Luton and how much farther was it. The cobbler, for that is what the man was, said that he was going the right way and might he enquire what his business in Luton was about. The giant, glad of a rest and a chat, told him exactly why he was going. This alarmed the cobbler who thought his own house might be buried too with this huge barrow of earth. He was a quick thinker and he tipped out his sack for the giant to see all the shoes needing repair that he was taking home to work on. He said: "I don't rightly know how many miles it is sir, but I have worn out all these shoes walking this far". The giant, who was now tired and thirsty, thought perhaps it was not a good idea after all, and he tipped the whole lot out beside the track and went home. So the quick witted cobbler saved the town and the mountainous pile of earth became green and wooded and was called "the Clappers" maybe "Cobblers" would have been a better name!

Both the Clappers and Pegsdon hills, which are next in line to the east, are covered in lovely wild thyme, rock roses, cowslips, quaking grass, orchids in spring, scabious, knapweed, marjoram and cow parsley in the summer, to name just a few. Flowers are not the only wild things; pheasants are always to be found in Pegsdon woods. They take off when disturbed, with a huge noise of whirring wings and raucous cries. Very satisfying for the dogs who get even more excited than usual, becoming once again totally deaf to our calls. This is a rather muddy walk and we try to keep it for dry weather or otherwise we have a major clean up job to do when we get home. They have such huge feet and the clay soil attaches to their fur and forms lozenges between their toes and up their legs, which is a devil to shift.

One day last week Tom found a new spot in the bottom chestnut paling fence where there was a slightly bigger gap and they both escaped into the wood. It was fifteen minutes at least before it dawned on me that everything was unnaturally quiet! I went to investigate and found no dogs. I stood and listened and was rewarded by the sound of distant crashing about. They had obviously been free for quite a while because I coaxed them back through the same gap without much trouble. Tom had a thorn in his pad I soon discovered which might have helped! He made a terrible fuss, walking with a heavy limp and holding his paw up pathetically. He made even more fuss when I was getting it out!

I was not best pleased at having to spend more time reinforcing the fence, as I had invited the members of my garden society, the NCCPG, to come and, I hoped, admire the garden. This was less than a week ahead and there was still much to do (not including emergency repairs to the fence). It was painfully obvious that now they had tasted the delights of freedom they were going to find new gaps everywhere and a major re-think was urgent. Meanwhile we kept them out of the lower garden.

I tried to continue with my weeding and tidying but the rain beat me time after time. Phillip Eden on local radio said we had had five inches in a week and still it came down. By Saturday everything was bowed over with the weight of water and I was getting drenched just walking along the path with the drooping plants eagerly shedding their watery cargos down my legs at the slightest touch. In spite of the weather about twenty keen gardeners turned up and trudged bravely round with wellies, macs and brollies. They even managed to say complimentary things about it but I was disappointed, as it would have looked so much better in sunshine! I had put the inevitable plant table up in the garage and they clustered round, and dripped, a mug of tea in one hand and a bag of treasures in the other, chatting about our gardening disasters and triumphs. I had lots of plants left over but they could come out again in few weeks time when we would throw the gates open again, this time aid of the National Garden Scheme.

Several weeks passed; we added chicken wire to the base of the fence where the cattle wire did not reach and relaxed again. They were behaving better on walks to the park and I was actually enjoying taking them. Robyn had given them a few short sharp lessons - with the help of their choke chains - reminders about walking to heel. Once they have been to the end of our short road and back with her, they are behaving like angels, leads slack and noses hardly ahead at all. Although she really makes them yelp until they behave, they do not bear a grudge, they adore her and when she arrives for lunch, as she does several times a week, they give her a huge welcome. Gill nearly dislocates his back wagging his whole body.

Of course this state of affairs could not last. I was returning from a walk, nearly home in fact, when, rounding a corner, there on the other side of the road was a large lady with a small dog on an extending lead who barked defiantly at them. Something it said upset the hooligans and they barked furiously back and lunged across the road, taking me by surprise and pulling me off my feet and flat on my face. Not unnaturally, somewhere during this spectacular tumbling act I let go of them and the little dog fled, extending lead doing just that, with them in hot pursuit. The young lady made swift and painful contact with a lamppost but she still hung on bravely to the lead. I stood up, my knees were stinging, but everything was still in one piece and working, thank goodness - I was just furious with the dogs. The other owner was cross and hurting too, but, as I had suffered even more then she had, I suspect she was slightly mollified. She probably thought that if I could not control my huge bully dogs

I deserved my bruises! I quickly captured Gill but Tom was too worried about my intentions with regard to him to come near; he trailed us a few yards behind, his lead getting filthy and scratched until we reached home. I then opened the garden gate and stood back as he shot past me. I pushed Gill after him, having removed his lead, and then let myself into the house to lick my wounds before letting them indoors. I did not scold them too much. For all I knew, whatever the little dog had said might have been such an insult that their reaction was justified!

We have a very doggy road and, as part of their lead training, David takes the two of them on a circuit most evenings. Number five, next door, has a very well behaved black Labrador Bitch who only speaks when she is spoken to! Number three is overflowing with Samoyeds, five of them, all very beautiful, Persil white and gorgeous. They are show dogs, with impressive rosettes proudly displayed. Ours always bark furiously at them but they seldom appear to even notice their existence, such is their breeding! Number one is dogless, number two has a well built German Shepherd named 'Lucky' which is precisely what you would not be if you ventured into his garden. He hears the boys approaching and his reaction is quite terrifying, he hurls himself at the six-foot wall, barking furiously and seeming about to appear over the top. Ours bark insults back and leap at the outside, pulling David all over the place and making sure that the whole neighbourhood is aware of their approach. The next canine residents are at number six; two more German Shepherds, an elderly chap and a youngster who is learning to be a guard dog too and takes his duties very seriously, which means another very noisy encounter. It is time to come back on our side, past first a Doberman Bitch, who is usually indoors and only sometimes seen. Another dogless residence is next, before the two friendly King Charles take up the chorus. Next door to us at number nine, there are two cats, who get chased if they are rash enough to set foot in our garden. Jean, my friend and neighbour, often puts any left over cat food in their bowl outside the front door and, if the boys smell it on the way back to our front door, David has another arm wrenching battle to prevent them doing a clean-up job. They love cat food and so do hedgehogs who are the intended recipients - if they get a chance to enjoy any of it!

Because of the chance of a mouthful of this ambrosia, if they ever manage to escape out of our front door they are round at Jean's door in a trice and sometimes they find it open - what joy! They bound in, hoover up any bowls of food found on the kitchen floor, scattering any cats that might be there. Only when they are satisfied that there is nothing left to eat do they bother to be sociable and greet Jean, who is actually quite fond of them, I cannot imagine why. They give her a quick sniff and a wag, then rush round her house into every open door, and then a quick inspection of the back garden completes the exercise, which is conducted at top speed and takes about two minutes. In fact, by the time I have realised that they have gone, so has Jean's cat food and cats, who have taken refuge somewhere, and the dogs are on their way back!

Occasionally when they feel more adventurous and go visiting all along the road, we pursue them just in case they upset anyone or leave unpleasant evidence of their visit. One day David dashed off in pursuit and as he ran in a straight line, while they zigzagged to and fro, he reached number six at the same time as they did. Oh what fun! Their garage was open and so was the door from it into the house. In they trooped (can two troop?) and went all round the house looking for the dogs (he presumed) but mercifully they had gone out for a walk or murder might have been done. The lady of the house captured them and led them out to a very embarrassed David, who apologised and brought them home in disgrace yet again.

Later on, when I recounted their escapade to my mother, she recalled that she had once been out with all five Gordon Setters in the pre-war days of almost nil traffic. They were walking beautifully with her, without leads, when suddenly the ringleader, Peter, decided to investigate an open front door and trotted in, followed by the others, round the occupied breakfast table he went, up the stairs, had a quick rekkie, down again and out before the astonished residents had had time to take in what was happening! A better story than mine I felt!

David and I are neither of us tidy by nature, things get just put down to be sorted later, but when they were very small and stole anything and everything we got much better. If we did not put the shoes, scarf and gloves, duster, whatever, away, it got chewed. Sadly as they improved we reverted to our bad habits and now and then when they have a relapse we are presented with a mitten that had recently been a glove, a wellington boot with an attractively scalloped top or a peep toe. Odd boots matched up as best we can are worn for gardening to the amusement of our friends. Food accidentally left out is spotted - or rather smelled out and rapidly dealt with. A butter dish or a full bowl of cat food left unattended when the phone rings is targeted instantly and lifted down to floor level without spilling a drop, then they both tuck in, gobbling it up like lightning before they are discovered. They give themselves away with the merry rattling of their identity tags against the metal bowl, but I am always too late to rescue any food; just a scolding is all they get and that is water off a duck's back. They are equally swift at taking the actual tin of food while I am downstairs feeding the cats. Gill licks it out as clean as a whistle but Tom gets frustrated and chews it up to get at the last licking in the bottom.

Chapter 7

D.I.Y. BOARDING KENNEL

Holidays and animals are difficult; if you cannot take them with you, or board them with friends, you are faced with the considerable expense of boarding kennels. When we had the boys we were intending to park them with Robyn and John or Robert and Rachael and repay them by looking after Jason and Sasha or Max in return. After the first experiment at Robyn's and the chicken episode, it was obvious that we were stuck with the expensive solution. The cats are well organised, however. My neighbour Jean and I have a reciprocal arrangement, as we both have three moggys and we look after each other's when necessary. Robyn and John take their dogs with them when they go away and bring their cats to us. To just add cats to the household would cause open warfare, with our unsociable, spoilt felines giving no quarter. Quite apart from that, there is the worry of them escaping and this would be too much to cope with. John, the practical handy man, is always full of ideas and he had made a splendid collapsible "A" frame kennel which we erect inside the garage for the duration of the cats' stay. It consists of five sections, two rectangular ones 10' x 6' and three triangular 6' x 6'. It has a small partition at one end with a door into it and an internal door into the main part from it, to foil any escape plans the visitors might have. One of the triangular sections fits at each end and the third one is the partition. The two main sides are joined at the top by hinges so that it can be collapsed easily and stored flat against the garage wall. When it is in use it occupies over half the double garage and gives the visitors plenty of space. A generous plywood box with hinged lid and front door is the bedroom and various toys are suspended from the mesh sides. The bedroom is sturdy enough to sit on and give the cats a cuddle and they can escape inside it away from unwelcome attentions and be really cosy among the blankets and cushions if it is cold. An old rug on the floor completes the set up. For entertainment our cats take turns to leer and jeer at the visitors through the wire. Puska spends practically all day on the garage half loft; she is the self-appointed early warning system should there be a breakout. Tabatha is the guard on the ground and Linka the commandant, who just puts in the odd visit to make sure the other two are not slacking. The dogs are allowed to say hello through the wire when they have their leads on, but more than a few seconds gets them so excited that they jump up the sides and actually made a small tear in the wire mesh with their huge paws, so they are now banned completely; this makes the garage and its occupants the most fascinating place in the world of course! Inevitably they get free now and then and rush in to visit. Robyn's cats are well used to her dogs and they sit on the bedroom box and out-stare the dogs, totally unmoved by their excitement. It has another use - when we have garden open days, we can pen the dogs in it and leave the garage open so that they can be "oo-ed" and "ah-ah-ed" over without escaping through the open garden gates. We add a couple of marrow bones to keep them entertained and everyone is happy. Only Poodle people recognise what they are; our unique barbering style is a good disguise and Standard Poodles are few and far between in this area.

One of their first 'Garden Open' experiences illustrates what a total menace they are. On their early morning run in the top garden they decided to have a frog hunt. We have a large population of frogs. With three ponds to breed in they do very well, in fact one year when we cleaned one pond out we counted over a hundred in the mud at the bottom. We put them in buckets until it was all sweet and clean again, then tipped them into the border to find their own way back, eating a few slugs en-route with a bit of luck. Although cleaning the pond is a mucky job and the black ooze at the bottom smells terrible, I never mind; clad in waders, old clothes and rubber gloves, I get stuck in - literally. Then I spread the mud on the garden before refilling it and watching with satisfaction as the clear water creeps up

On guard duty.

the sides again. But I digress. This morning in question was the day before the garden open day; I got out of bed and looked out of the window. To my horror I saw them both on the border, heads down, nosing along and flattening everything in their path ! I dashed out in my nightie to find that they had surprised a frog somewhere and had pursued it into the border, where they were pushing and shoving each other to get next turn at prodding it into another leap. They had not hurt it, frogs having evil tasting skin apparently, but the poor thing was exhausted. I picked it up and put it into the pond well out of their reach, then having shouted at them for being on the garden I examined the mayhem. Many stems were bent and broken, flowers were trampled and a few small holes had been dug for good measure. I quickly got dressed. About twenty feet of border demolished. What on earth could I do? The dogs were staying well way from me, romping on the far side of the lawn, so I got busy with thin green split cane and string and for over an hour I splinted bent stems, removed broken ones and smoothed the earth, filling holes and raking paw prints. It looked a bit better but not a lot. Then I had a brain wave. I made a notice headed "Wildlife in the garden". Then I listed the birds, hedgehogs, frogs, squirrels etc., and finished with "poodlus vulgaris nigra" - a destructive species, addicted to digging and chasing other wild life through the flower beds, at present imprisoned in the garage! I mounted this on hardboard and nailed it to a stake - at least the visitors would be able to smile at my bad luck!

Sunday dawned bright and the forecast was not bad, so we felt cheerful enough as we put out deck chairs, umbrellas and trestle tables, some for the plant sale and some for refreshments. The mat and marrow bones in situ in the cat pen, we thought we were ready. David offered to take the pair for a good run before the home action started at 11.00 a.m. He was back again by 10.45 a.m. and already the early birds were queuing in the road, hoping for a plant table bargain. We did not want to shut the boys up until the last minute as they would be there a long time, so we put them in the lower garden with Jo who was down there, still setting things up. Suddenly there is a shout for help! Tom has jumped the fence into the neighbours' garden whose house is on the main road. There is no way I could get into this garden to retrieve him. I had to shin over the fence via my compost heap, (all in my nice clean clothes), into the adjoining garden, through their bottom fence, not difficult because it is full of gaps, to where his Nibs was investigating this lovely new territory. Because of our unique position in our cul-de-sac, we have five gardens adjacent to our boundaries. Once I had found Tom he came to me quite happily, but I now had the problem of how to get back. There was no compost heap to climb onto this side and my only route was up the lane behind the houses, into the next road and back along it to our turning - probably a quarter of a mile to get back to where I started and by now it was two minutes to eleven o'clock! The queue viewed me with interest as I pulled Tom down the drive - I had no lead, so I just had to hang onto his collar. Gill was already penned up and I thankfully pushed the sinner in with his brother and shot the bolt. David had only just found out what had happened and was about to come and meet me.

Flap over, we let the visitors come in; there were around two hundred of them and in four hours there were very few plants left and lots of happy people carrying pots of treasure home, tummies full of tea and cake and hands full of carrier bags and boxes. Next we have to go into reverse and put all the tables, deck chairs, left over plants etc. away for next time. The food was divided between the helpers. The organisers of the charity which was benefiting from the gate money were eagerly counting the lolly and asking for a repeat performance next year - hey-ho!

Towards the end, when things had quietened down and only a handful of visitors were left, we released the dogs; they rushed joyfully about greeting everyone, with much embarrassing crotch - sniffing which I pretended not to notice. They were soon distracted by the cake and biscuits and managed to steal some before they were stopped. Unabashed, they returned to enjoy the fuss and compliments showered on them by doggy people. They very soon came to associate garden visitors with fuss and food; in fact I have teased people by saying "when they look at you what they actually see is a potential source of chocolate biscuits". They perfected the trick of sitting angelically in front of someone in the act of conveying biscuit to mouth, not saying a word or moving an inch, just watching the biscuit to and fro and dribbling until the poor person being targeted is also being encouraged by other people: "Oh, give him a bit, don't be mean" etc. They always did very well! They only get human biscuits on open days and they really make the most of it! We raised the fence with eighteen inches of netting along the top, next day.

Feeding the cats on the washing machine is becoming more unsatisfactory by the day. The boys smell the food, leap up and steal the bowl plus contents, the moment I open the door. I stalled this trick temporarily by telling them NOT to jump up to the cats, at the same whacking a rolled newspaper viciously on the door. There is no need to actually hit them with it, the sight and sound is enough to distract them from their mischief. However, the cats are so traumatised by the banging of papers and the rushing of clumsy bodies through their haven, that I must take further steps to ensure the return of a more peaceful existence. After all they are old ladies now and poor Puska is on the verge of a nervous breakdown!

Another unnerving trick Tom plays is to take two or three steps on his back legs while passing by and give a wet kiss to whoever is in residence in the basket. I could not be cross because he was only being affectionate but the cats are not impressed, and wet fur is angrily licked dry and groomed into shape again.

I decided that the top of the broom cupboard would always be out of reach of anything shorter than a giraffe, the only problem was that, although Tabatha and Puska could jump up there and often did, Linka at seventeen years old would not manage it. I solved it by fixing the children's old bunk ladder to the side of the cupboard; it

All gone.

was just the right length and the cats lost no time in using it. What remained of their basket I put up there and we christened the new refuge "the penthouse". I had to get the small steps to reach the top to change their blanket or whatever, but that was easy enough and for a while peace reigned again.

Ready for visitors.

Chapter 8

AWKWARD ADOLESCENTS

Visits by Robyn were frequent and we went walking together with the four dogs most weeks, but visits from Robert and Max were much less often and the reception they received was a mixed one. Robert the strict disciplinarian earned much worried wagging and submissive posturing; no jumping up was attempted and, if very dominant Max was with him, poor Gill invariably wet himself in his anxiety to please and placate growly Max, who, having received the homage he considered his due, would settle down in the best spot and ignore them. This business of leaking when nervous beset Gill until he was well over a year old and it was very hard on the hall carpet. Fortunately the light there is not too good and the fact that the constant mopping up has caused a colour change is not obvious, I hope!

On one of these visits, Robert and Rachael had come over to give us a hand in the garden and it was Tom not Gill who had a field day. They seem to know that I particularly want them to behave well when Robert is around as he has such a low opinion of us, and of course they do the opposite! During the winter months their route from door to gate across the grass had turned the area into something resembling the goal mouth of a football pitch. The lawn was so badly churned up that we decided to put a double row of paving stones in the grass along this rat run and Robert had promised to give us a hand. The first thing Tom did was to knock over and smash a new mug. It had been left on the steps after a coffee break; admittedly it was not a good place to put it, but it was well tucked into the side and he was just chasing madly about as usual. Soon after that there was a huge, wet commotion and he had not stopped at having a drink from the fish pond, he had gone in for a swim! Another delay and diversion, when he shook generously over all of us several times before disappearing into the bottom garden with Gill and Max. We were getting on with the stone laying and not taking too much notice of them when I thought it had been rather a long time since we had seen them. Max had come back but the other two were digging holes - like us, they said - in the onion bed this time. Embryo onions, earth and stones were being showered backwards onto the lawn much faster than we could have done it; they already had a lovely hole you could lose a bucket in and they were still at it hammer and tongs. Two pairs of back legs were spread out and front paws were shooting the earth out behind them at lightning speed. It was with lightning speed that they took off to escape my wrath! I chased them across the grass, verbally committing them to the tortures of hell. It had no impression whatever on them! During this excitement Max was lying near Robert as good as gold. Why are our dogs such delinquents? None of the others dig at all, neither do they jump anything more than three feet high, whereas ours can clear a five barred gate from a standing start and have given us heart attacks when they have sailed over barbed wire fences higher than that.

On days like this I reflect how much easier it would have been with only one dog who would then have related to us, instead of to his brother, against us, as so often seems to be the case. But I change my mind when I come upon them unexpectedly as they quietly romp together, ear chewing and play biting or wrestling over a sock. I caught them the other day with a pair of David's boxer shorts; they had each managed to get their head through a leg and were caught, heads together, looking as if they were wearing frilly bonnets, pulling each other to and fro in their attempts to escape. I rushed for my camera but as usual the flash took too long to warm up and by the time it was ready the game was over. I rescued the pants, scolded them for stealing them, and left them to their games. The summer is marching on, they are nearly nine months old and huge - surely they are going to stop growing soon.

In a short two months we are taking them with us to Cornwall.

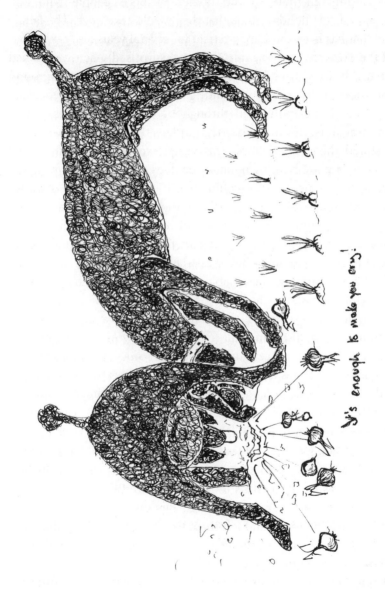

Digging in the onion bed.

The prospect of this fills me with dread. We are booked to spend three nights en-route in the homes of B&B people who had indicated in the holiday guide that they would take dogs. The family hotel that has been our happy retreat for several years also takes dogs and the owners were very intrigued and surprised when we booked as usual, but with two large canines too. We usually have a ground floor room with a balcony and garden door, so we requested this again. Plants purchased throughout the holiday, at the small interesting nurseries and wonderful gardens that abound down there, are stored there, but I knew this year I would have to forgo the pleasures of plant hunting because the dogs would be occupying the plant space in the car and would smash any horticultural treasures with their restless black paws. I thought of putting some on the roof rack, but over three hundred miles of relentless wind and weather would not do them much good either! Because my garden is so special to me, any plants I buy these days are also special or unusual and almost certainly unavailable nearer home. I decided to be strong-minded and not buy any.

Our departure date for Cornwall was mid-September, and we began to step up discipline and training as the weeks rushed by. The general behaviour of certain animals was not up to a standard acceptable to our unsuspecting hosts. The business of not coming to a call or whistle when on a walk was their most worrying fault. Robert suggested that, as they obviously competed with each other over speed and hunting skills, if we only released one at a time, whichever one was free would not have so much temptation on his own and therefore might return when called. We tried it; all that really happened was that the captive one nearly pulled David's arm off in his attempts to follow his brother, while the free one galloped off into the distance as usual, appearing not only to enjoy his brother's distress but to be spurred on by it!

We persevered for a couple of weeks and then abandoned the idea in favour of each of us having a dog on a long rope, about thirty feet long, and a pocket full of rewards. We had replaced liver with chocolate biscuits (less messy) and, taking care to stay far enough apart to prevent the two ropes being tangled together, we would wait for our dog to be interested in a smell or whatever and then call him. He did not come, of course, so we repeated the command and gave the rope a tug. When there was still no response we hauled the dog to us and scolded him before repeating the exercise, over and over again, each with our own dog. On the rare occasions when he did come, a biscuit was awarded. Our patience was rewarded to some degree after seemingly endless lessons, at least they came sometimes when called. This finally paid off and by the time the holiday weeks arrived we had made definite progress. Not enough to trust them on foreign territory but we felt that once we arrived in Cornwall we would at least be able to let them run free on the beach.

We also had to bath and cut the dogs, both to make them look attractive and to reduce the amount of mud or sand they could convey on their persons into the car and other people's rooms. It takes about an hour to bath them, including filling and emptying the bath. We have joined the hoses from the hot and cold taps in the utility room to make a 'mixer' hose and we feed it through the cat flap to the bath. This is watched with wary interest, being the least popular part of the performance, and it can take a few minutes to capture a dog and pull the reluctant object to the bath. David clamps an arm round his chest and another round his tummy and lifts him in, while I stand by to field the odd leg that gets left behind. During the exercise all three of us get soaked to the skin. We prepare ourselves by donning old tee shirts, shirts and flip-flops. When the autumn and winter come we shall have to wear our walking wet-weather gear, trousers, wellies - the lot. Once the dog is in the bath it gives in and stands patiently while we scoop water over it, to wet it before putting on lavish amounts of supermarket family shampoo. We make sure that one of us has a hand through its choke chain, there have been premature escapes before now! The rinsing

"I don't want a bath!" *"Well you're getting one!"*

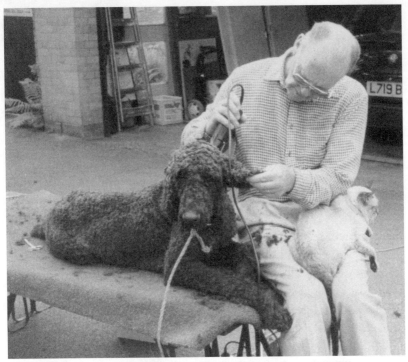

Tabatha getting in on the act at clipping time.

follows and finally we put the hose on again for a clean rinse before we let him go. He always shakes several times, which gets rid of a lot of the water; the rest is towelled off but first the other dog is given the same treatment. The water gets very soupy but we try to alternate which we bath first to even it up. It seems to work, they are both soft and cuddly to touch instead of wiry, and they smell gorgeous. They love being towelled and push each other to get all our attention. The floor gets wetter as they get dryer, as the towels get wet we spread them on the floor, both to dry feet and the floor before the whole lot goes into the washing machine. The utility room has a high tide mark of splashes from coat shaking at around waist high on all four sides - door, window, wall, boiler, washing machine, at least when this is wiped I have a cleaning job done too!

While I am clearing up, they are outside going absolutely crackers; the experience excites them tremendously and they tear round, chasing and ambushing each other and finishing off their drying in the process. We put the cover back on the bath once it is emptied and assemble the cutting paraphernalia on top (extension lead, cutter, brushes, scissors and collars). We only have to call them once, then they dash there, up on the table both trying to be first; we usually start with Gill because Tom waits more patiently. Gill keeps jumping up and upsetting Tom if we do it the other way round. We start down their back, mowing great swathes from neck to tail; they love it and stand as good as gold, which is just as well with the acreage there is to cover on each of them; the only part they hate is having their feet done, for some reason. I usually do that with scissors while David is mowing elsewhere. After about forty-five minutes we have a handsome dog and a pile of black wool which is too short to be any good for spinning and I put it on the compost heap; quite a lot is blown away and dispersed round the garden anyway. If only it would last longer, because in no time they are looking curly again - like Persian lamb instead of chenille velvet.

With only a few days to go, Tom with perfect timing cuts his dew pad rather badly and has to be bandaged to stop them both from an around the clock, licking campaign, stopping only to eat and exercise. Once bandaged there was a new challenge, how quickly could they unbandage it? By the time Saturday came it was improving but still open, and the battle to keep it clean and covered had to continue.

Packing for the dogs was a new experience. A twenty kilo sac of doggy muesli, drinking water for the journey, water and food bowls, two towels for muddy feet, chews, poopascoop and poly bags, it all took up a huge amount of room, and there were the dogs themselves too! We did not use the dog guard; they soon discovered that a good shove would dislodge it and we had not got around to having a permanent one fitted! We were going to regret this; we put a waterproof sheet on the boot floor with a rug on top and their now ridiculously small 'bed' rugs on the top of that, because they were a symbol of bedtime and a bit of home. Our own packing had to be squeezed into the back seat and included, as well as a large suitcase each, wellies, wet weather jackets and trousers, two bulky wet suits, a first aid box and picnic food. The surf boards were pushed under the rug in the boot; they are wooden "belly boards" and have provided us with such enormous fun all our married life, that they must know the way to Cornwall by now. They look outdated on the beach, but we still speed past the other surfers on their polystyrene rafts, much to their amazement. While I checked this incredible mix of luggage, David took them for a quick run in the park and returned within the hour without incident, praise be!

Chapter 9

WE'RE ALL GOING ON A SUMMER HOLIDAY

We are off! Our destination tonight is an inn in the Cotswolds, a deliberately short journey to allow for any unforeseen problems! I have done and redone the inside of the car and at last everything is in, including the dogs, who have watched the performance from the kitchen window and were delirious when they found that they were coming too! I had tried to put the bits and pieces of essential equipment (like dog biscuits and lunch for us) on the top. It was hard to keep the dogs in the back, as they have watched us depart without them on our way to work etc. so many times and they were wild with joy and excitement. They nearly wagged themselves in half!

By lunch time we had arrived and found the inn. We had so much time we took off again in search of a picnic spot. You have probably noticed that picnics spots and penny country abound when you are not looking for them, but once you start looking all the fields have high hedges or nettles or cattle or all three; gates bristle with barbed wire and the ground is a quagmire. At last we found it, a stubble field with an open gate and no mud to get stuck in. We pulled up, spread our rug and, while I prepared the food, David walked the boys round the field, then he attached the leads to the car before we settled down out of range to enjoy our lunch, disturbed only by a passing panda car whose occupants hovered for a long minute to make sure we were harmless before driving on.

Replete, we drove on to Bibury where we stopped by a trout stream, put on our wellies and took the dogs for a decent walk along this stream, through woods and on into a stubble field. Everything looked quiet and empty, so we let them free. We foolishly thought that, as they had no idea where they were, they would stay within sight of us; no chance, they just took off into the distance!! They did come back eventually and, after covering several circular miles round and round the field as we just strolled across it, we managed to recapture them at the far gate before we ventured further into unknown territory. It was just as well we did because the next field was full of bullocks; curious as bullocks are they escorted us to the next gate. The boys were not at all sure they liked this and walked very close without pulling. The next hazard was the area by the gate we now had to get through. It had been churned into a mass of squelchy potholes. We thought of the bedroom waiting for us at the inn and did our best to pick our way through without their curly wool collecting too much mud, but they get balls of mud between their toes which are very hard to shift. I have often wished they could wear wellies too! We found our way back to the car and finished the afternoon exploring some of the lovely Costwold villages. We loved Burford with its hilly high street of terraced houses and shops, every other one being an antique shop! We passed through cosy undulating fields with yellow ochre stone cottages dotted about among small woods and hedges, a very pastoral landscape which soothed our senses and made us feel that our holiday had begun. We started to relax.

It was 5.00 p.m. before we got back to the inn, and we were beginning to feel very hungry. We parked at the back and left the dogs in the car while we introduced ourselves. We were shown to our bedroom, all pink roses and lace, and we just looked at each other, there was no need for words! In fact we need not have worried, the boys were marvellous. We waited until the landlord had gone before we took them in, because when we booked we had said we had two poodles, fearing that we might be refused if we disclosed how big they were. I certainly would not want two unknown monsters like them in my pretty bedroom! The way in was through the back door and immediately up the stairs to the bedrooms. We reached ours unobserved, although the tramp of heavy feet was impossible to hide. They pulled us up, weaving about to smell everything, but they did not bark and we were soon inside our room with the door shut.

David fetched their bowls, food and bed mats and we used an empty plastic food sack as a table cloth on the floor in the en-suite. They were much too excited to eat much and we just let them sniff around while we unpacked, showered and changed. They found their bed rugs and flopped down like children who had found their precious teddies. We too flopped down (on the bed) to read until the evening meal was ready.

We put them back in the car while we went in to dinner, and again we were unobserved. We were starving and made short work of the excellent pub-grub. Soon we were all back in the bedroom with the TV on and two happy dogs content to be with us. They do not sleep in our room at home and we wondered if they would try to come onto the bed with us, as it was the lace bedcover that worried me, but all was well, the only problem being that now we had established that this was our room they barked furiously at other guests passing the door.

They woke us about 7.00 a.m. by prodding us with their leathery noses and did not give up until we made a move. Reluctantly we dressed, lay-ins are a thing of the past! After we had packed up we took them for a short stroll down the road, before shutting them in the car and going in search of food. We were chatting to the proprietor over our full English breakfast and he told us of a circular walk of about three miles starting just opposite down Bow-wow lane! It could be just what we wanted to settle them down before more travelling and confinement in the boot again. It could have been a very pleasant walk, past a canal, lakes and fields, but it soon began to drizzle and then to really rain, in fact it became a deluge. Our jackets were waterproof but we had not bothered with our waterproof trousers, so our legs were soon soaked, and the dogs could have benefited from a spin dryer by the time we reached the car. We towelled them till the worst was absorbed then changed our trousers and felt much better. Crewkerne was our next destination and we drove through the rain all the morning. We had to picnic in the car as it was still raining; it was pretty steamy in there too with damp dogs and damp clothes!

It was still fairly early and when we saw a yellow "Garden Open" sign, David dropped me off again, and once again I was the only visitor. It was mainly a rose garden and well past its best, but I chatted to the owner and in the course of our garden chat I asked him if he knew where we could give the dogs a run. "Certainly," he said, "the field behind the garden is mine too and it is fenced, they could run there" - Super! I went out to the car and told David the good news, because it had stopped raining at last too. They had a jolly good run around, the grass being very long they were soaked again. The field was separated from the rose garden by a stream and they had a paddle in that (just to make sure their feet were clean) they implied. In the long grass we found a pair of diminutive swimming trunks and a kitchen knife, and they found a football sized foam ball in a bright bilious green. This they refused to relinquish and, when I finally got possession of it, it was minus a big chunk and useless as a ball, so we let them continue to play with it, chasing each other for ownership. More chunks came out all the time until there was nothing left except small pieces of foam scattered in the grass. David took them back to the car while I returned the knife and trunks. I owned up about the ball and thanked the owner. He was glad to see the knife again but the trunks - his grand son's - had not been missed.

We set off in search of our new 'digs'. This time the book had given us an address - "well behaved dogs welcome" - with a splendid description of a bungalow with marvellous gardens and comfortable rooms with bath and TV, just the job we thought. We found it easily, perched high above the road with a precipitous drive and small car park below. As before we put the car with dogs in as inconspicuous spot as possible before going to make our introductions.

The interior was decorated in what I believe is called colonial style, very reminiscent of a Somerset Maughan novel: it was absolutely choc-a-block with knick-knacks, little tables loaded with pottery were everywhere, plants in serpentine cane containers flowed from corners, and still more pottery stood on the floor. A stuffed parrot studied us from in a cage, and above our heads a giant fan like an aircraft propeller gently revolved. As if that was not enough, the carpet that extended right up to the front door was cream!! We nearly died! How on earth were we going to get the excessively vigorous boys through this minefield without some expensive accident? The bedroom came as no surprise as it was equally cluttered, the carpet pale pink and everything very frilly including the loo and dressing table. We smiled bravely and made complimentary noises to our host, then the minute he left us on our own we moved the ornaments, the vases of dried flowers and the teas-maid to higher levels before we went back for the boys.

We had hoped to sneak them in unseen but unfortunately we met our host again on the doorstep just as we struggled to control two excited dogs who having been penned up for over an hour, had quite forgotten their fun in the field. Poor man, his face was a picture! They smelt decidedly "doggy" since their paddle and he too was expecting small dogs - these were very large and very damp - he obviously had grave doubts about letting them in at all ! All he could manage to say was "I thought they were poodles"! We explained that with our D.I.Y cutting, they did not look like poodles but they truly were, and they were very good!! (We had our fingers crossed!) We then thoroughly towelled their feet as we stood on the door step and took off our own shoes. He reluctantly stood aside and, with our hands through their collars and their front feet barely touching the ground, we half carried them through to the bedroom without any mishap. We put down their rugs and feeding bowls and were pleased to watch them tuck in. After yesterday's poor showing they were hungry. We followed the same pattern and put them in the car while we ate, then gave them another walk before bedtime, once again towelling their feet on the door step and shedding our wellies, before bringing them in again.

We were in bed and asleep when I suddenly jumped back to consciousness, woken by the sound of somebody heaving and retching! I shot out of bed, grabbed the paper David had been reading and shoved it under Gill's head in the nick of time!! He produced all his meal followed by chunks of foam ball. When I was sure he had got rid of all of it, I found a plastic carrier bag and put the loaded newspaper in it for disposal in the morning. David woke at this point and said "I hadn't finished reading that!" I crept back to bed, not amused, but thankful that the deep pile pink carpet, and my embarrassment, had both been spared. That was all the excitement over. Once again we gave them a quick walk before we shut them in the car, never to threaten the shag pile again. I am sure the owners were amazed and relieved that they had been so angelic, we certainly were! We imagined them both hurrying to examine the bedroom before we were halfway down the drive!

The last port of call on our leisurely journey west was to see a gardening friend of mine who lives in a marvellous spot just on the hem of Dartmoor near Newton Abbot. She had foolishly persuaded us to spend a night with her, as she has two well-behaved Collies of her own and the prospect of entertaining the boys did not bother her at all. She also has seven pedigree rabbits and six ponies, quite a menagerie in fact. We decided it would be wise to aim for Dartmoor and have our picnic and walk before we landed on Anne's doorstep.

We hoped to get rid of some of their energy before they were introduced. We managed to get lost in the lanes around Holme, finding some precipitous hills in the process with one in four gradients and exciting hairpins. We found Watersmeet eventually, just as the morning's showery rain was giving way to cotton wool clouds and enough blue to make that sailor's trousers; however we did not trust it, and picnicked immediately before it changed its mind and rained again. We chained the dogs to the car as before and they settled down without making a cats cradle of the chain and having to be rescued and unravelled before they hanged themselves.

We could see the little rocky river rushing noisily along, as clear as crystal and a little further down in the slightly more sheltered valley that it had carved out for itself over the centuries a few rowans were growing laden with red berries, looking marvellous in the sunshine. It was just the kind of scene you wish you could roll up like a magic carpet and put down in your own garden. You would need the sheep too to keep the grass mown right up to the artistic boulders scattered around by some huge flood in a bygone age. The volume of water would also need a large pump, but I am only dreaming. It would not be practical to maintain, even if you had astronomical funds and some talented landscaper of the standard you see at Chelsea flower show, to do it for you. Some plants would get too big and swamp others, or die and leave gaps, while cutting the grass round the rocks would be fiddley to put it mildly! Far easier to admire nature's own masterpiece.

A quick walk through the heather with the boys on leads, to settle our lunch, came next. No chance of a free run for them with sheep, ponies and even a few cattle scattered around half hidden in the scrub. They were very excited by all the new smells and we had our exercise just holding on to them! We repacked some of the stuff in the car and while we were not looking they stole and ate half a cut loaf, they also ate the bag!

We set off for Anne's farm and found her very lame because of a bad hip, but struggling manfully to get her large garden into some sort of order for an open day next week. It was still only mid afternoon so, better late than never, we got stuck in and helped her. David attacked the wet grass with the flymo, making mint sauce as he went and I tried to weed the very overgrown rose bed. Our dogs quickly made friends with the Collies and were happy just wandering about.

Not only was Anne trying to get the garden sorted out, she had a date next day to show two of her ponies at Widdicombe Fair. I have only the sketchiest knowledge of horses, remembered from a very short riding career about fifteen years ago that was brought to an end by my hip problems. Both my daughters ride well and love horses, so the jargon is not unfamiliar, but I had never groomed a horse before. I was going to learn fast. I found myself with a brush in my hand trying to get the dust out of the coat of a gorgeous yearling called Jewel, who was not impressed by my unsure efforts and bit me. Not badly, just enough to make me yelp! Anne was busy in the next stall with a larger, good natured mare called Fen, and on hearing me squeak became very anxious as dear Jewel had given her a nip the day before and this is just not done! Poor Anne is not able to dodge and anticipate as fast as she did, hampered by her hip, and as a result was getting worried about handling Madam the next day at the fair. I had progressed to mane and tail plaiting and was getting on better. At last Anne said we were done and we went in for a cuppa; brushing dusty ponies is a very thirsty job.

David in the meantime had finished the grass and came with the dogs to find us. The prize rabbits are safely housed in the stables too, and Tom and Gill, noses twitching furiously, soon found them and glued themselves to the wire netting that was keeping them apart. They could not believe their eyes; this smell, so familiar from many walks at home, had suddenly taken shape and was there nonchalantly munching just a few inches away. The rabbits were used to the Collies, and as the dogs were too overcome to say a word, they were not alarmed and carried on eating while the boys watched, completely mesmerised. Although both of them are such a menace chasing everything that moves, they are puzzled if it does not move! The ponies we had just groomed were in the next door stalls and, when they put their heads over the half-doors to have a look at the visitors, the dogs just looked back!

We asked Anne where we could take them for a proper run, and she directed us through the field behind the farmhouse, where the rest of the horses were peacefully grazing, and into woods behind and down beside a little stream. It sounded lovely but through the horse field?? She assured us that her horses were not a bit nervous of dogs, in fact the biggest pony appropriately called 'Evil' would chase them if they showed any tendency to do likewise! Could this be the answer to teach Tom a lesson? Perhaps if he got a fright he might change his wicked ways, as he is actually quite a coward and will run away if anything shows any aggression to him. He was once chased a hundred yards or more by a Yorkie with whom he tried to take liberties! We laughed our socks off.

To return to the paddock, Tom is so fleet of foot we were not worried about Evil actually catching him and doing him a mischief! Poor Tom, we went through the gate and I closed it again, then we let them go. They went, like rockets barking with joy, to the far side where the horses were quietly grazing. The next moment it was as if the film had been put on rewind! Back they came, with Evil in hot pursuit; Gill came to us and tried to hide behind David, but Tom did three circuits of the field breaking all his previous records, with Evil just on his tail, before, panic stricken, he found the gate and cleared it with ease. It was a very quiet, thoughtful dog that finished the walk with us and he has been very wary of horses ever since. Now he will only do his barking, when he is safe on the other side of a fence or in the car. He is a reformed character but I wonder for how long?

Once back indoors we fed them and then smartened ourselves up, before taking Anne to the local "good grub" pub for a meal. We dared not leave them behind for fear of what they might think of doing to Anne's home, so we took them with us. They obviously got bored, and, while we consumed venison in red wine, the dogs ate the roll of poly bags we had ready in the pocket for poopa -scoop jobs, to make their point. But it was not until next day that we discovered the full extent of their activities! A quick walk up the lane with them when we got back was necessary. On leads of course, but they managed to dive into the hedge a few times after irresistible scents and had to be hauled out, dragging long trails of blackberry with them, stuck to their woolly backs. Then it was straight to bed for all of us. Tom managed to steal an opened cat food tin on the way through the kitchen and was very reluctant to give up his prize, we finally rescued it plus puncture holes and minus its contents, oh dear!

Our bedspread was white. On our bedspread was a strange triangular dark patch near one side. I investigated, it was muddy blood. While I investigated Tom obligingly went round to the other side of the bed and laid his chin on it to demonstrate how he did it, leaving a matching mark that side. He had cut his chin on the tin. He was having a good day.

Next morning I washed the bloody bits out, having confessed his crime to Anne, and then put the whole thing in the washing machine. Anne had to be away by 8.30 a.m. with the horses, so we helped with the final beauty treatments and fed the rabbits for her. We were very careful when we opened their cages as Tom and Gill were both taking a great interest, but we accomplished it without disaster and breathed again. The last task was to load the ponies into the horse box. In the meantime a gorgeous hunk of male called Simon had arrived in a Land-rover. He loaded them in for us. He had no worries about being bitten by stroppy Jewel, but Anne was not happy about her and we heard later that she had sold her. Such a pity, she was so beautiful, but that's life, perhaps her next owner taught her who was boss. We wished Anne good luck and waved her and the horses good-bye. Then we packed ourselves up, all ready to leave. When we opened the back near-side car door it was to discover that it was spread thinly but thoroughly with butter. The butter had been inside a plastic tub, inside a Tupperware container, inside the zipped up bag! Somehow, while we were in the pub they had opened the bag and chewed through both containers. The butter also coated the inside of the picnic bag and was liberally spread over the back seat and surrounding luggage. Our cases were inside the house thank heavens, but it was the radio, first aid box, wet suit bag and odds and ends that had suffered. In the darkness of the night before we had not seen the mess at all. They had really enjoyed themselves. To be philosophical, if it had to happen I suppose this was a good time, because at least we had a kitchen, hot water and detergent at our disposal! We made free with Anne's facilities and then wrote what we hoped was a humorous letter explaining what had happened. The only permanent damage was the Tupperware and butter tub, as we cleaned everything else fairly well and then, very behind schedule, took them for their walk, taking sadistic pleasure in going through the horse field again! Tom had to be dragged along, but the horses did not even raise their heads, for they had won and they knew it! Gill managed to cut his face and dripped blood all the way back to the car, but it soon stopped and we were past caring. It was nearly eleven o'clock before we finally got away!

We were very conscious of our grubby appearance as we approached our hotel. The last port of call with its gardening, horse grooming and de-buttering of the car had not improved my pale grey silky tracksuit and David looked equally scruffy with a large clear paw print in the middle of his back, Gill's artistic idea! This time we had been honest when we booked and had described the dogs as large Poodles. We were given our usual welcome and the boys were admired. We explained our appearance, blaming the dogs and then wondered if that had been wise in view of the fact that theses juvenile delinquents were going to be turning their attentions to Rose-in-Vale's furniture and fittings for the next ten days!!! Mr and Mrs Arthur remained fairly calm at the prospect and we said silent prayers that all would be well, without much hope of them being answered.

Chapter 10

CORNWALL

We discovered when we unpacked completely that, as well as poly bags and butter, they had found and eaten their complete holiday supply of biscuits. No wonder they were not hungry yesterday! Everybody knows that what goes in one end has to come out of the other, and if it does not you have problems. It was therefore with some anxiety that we monitored their bodily functions. We need not have worried, maybe the butter acted as a lubricant for the less digestible items. The plastic evidence appeared to prove their guilt, not that any proof was needed. We were relieved that they had come to no harm from their strange supper, and now all was passed, so to speak, the danger of 'accidents' in the bedroom was reduced. In fact that first night they slept as soundly as we did.

We were now on familiar ground and we established a regular routine straightaway. The days began with a cuppa soon after 7.00 a.m. which David usually made in our room. Then we prepared for the day according to the weather forecast and the view from the window. I would get our beach gear together and fill a coffee flask while David took them up to the horse field which is part of the hotel grounds. Both the resident horses were still in their stable at this hour and would watch with interest as David was towed at a smart pace past them. They ignored the horses altogether, the memory of Evil still fresh. Ten minutes was allowed for a mad rush around, to enjoy wonderful rabbit smells and horse traces. Once he could recapture them, David shut them in the car while we had a leisurely breakfast. The food at Rose-in-Vale is very good and not to be hurried! Once replete, we loaded the day's gear and departed for Perranporth, which has a huge beach, picturesque cliffs and sand dunes, not to mention good surf if the tide is right. Our sort of surfing, belly-boarding, is only possible when the tide is high. Not every day produces surf that

Perranporth

is any good and, with only nine days to play with, our potential frolic in the waves takes priority over everything else. The temperature, sun, rain or wind make no difference. If there are good waves we go in, our wet suits protecting us against the elements.

During the journey down we had bitterly regretted not having a secure barrier between 'their' area in the boot and the main body of the car. Now we were settled we kept everything not needed for the day's programme in our room. This cut out their fun and games, such as, nipping into the back seat the instant we left them and rapidly locating and consuming anything edible. The picnic bag was very vulnerable and we were forced to buy food on a daily basis instead of chopping up a loaf and having it with butter, cheese and tomatoes, keeping left over bits and pieces from one day to the next. It had to be pre-packed sandwiches or a pasty, bought just before we were going to eat it. My store of home grown tomatoes was untouched, as dogs don't like tomatoes, but apples and pears are worth chewing if one gets a bit peckish when 'they' have gone off in those ridiculous penguin suits.

Our first day was fine if not warm and we were as excited as a couple of kids at the first sight this year of Perran's three and a half miles of sand with the prospect of introducing Tom and Gill to it. First we paid a visit to the pet shop to replace the stolen biscuits, and found ourselves buying new collars too. The dogs are an awkward size, but here we found a red one for Tom and blue one for Gill, we were delighted. There were plenty of people on the beach in the late September sunshine and we kept them on leads until we were clear of the main picnic area. It was as well we did, as later excursions proved. They are extremely curious and when free would investigate every windbreak. Although they look friendly, they are so big, especially if you are sitting on the ground, that children are apt to panic and run away. Then they bark and give chase, thinking it is a game. Parents tended to get stroppy when their picnics are inspected and children frightened, and windbreaks are just right as tree substitutes!

Once all these hazards were behind us we gave them their freedom. They simply did not know what to do or where to go first; they zig-zagged, noses to the sand, then were distracted by other dogs who needed greeting and inspecting. Then they described wide circles around us, gaining confidence all the time in this strange new world. We walked diagonally towards the sea. The tide was low, so it was quite a way off, but we badly wanted to see their reaction to it and of course to assess the surf with a view to going in later on. The wet areas left by the retreating tide were super fun; they flew together through the ribbed sand throwing up plumes of water and not really noticing at all when the wet sand became very shallow sea.

Just a quick wee.

We fell about laughing when Tom dashed into about four inches of water and turned round to see if Gill was following, only to be swamped by a wave while his back was turned. He spun round to see where it had come from, then retreated to sandy safety, picking up his feet like a dressage pony. He clearly distrusted this big pond which chased him when he was not looking. For the rest of the day they were very wary and only splashed about in the very edge.

They drew the usual interest from the other doggy people on the beach, most of whom wanted to know what they were, as usual. Perran beach always has lots of dogs because it is one of a decreasing number of places which still make them welcome. Dog owners have brought the "no dogs" ban on themselves by being selfish and not cleaning up after their pets. Nevertheless the ban must surely make a difference in the future to tourist numbers, as dog owners make up quite a percentage of the visitors. We have ourselves driven in and straight out of quite a few worthwhile favourite spots when we have seen the dog ban sign, so others must surely do likewise.

How about some rock climbing?

By the time we had walked the full length of the beach and back it was time to find some lunch. We put their leads on and took them into the town, where we bought prawn sandwiches and a tide timetable - vital for our surf planning. The car was still just alongside the beach with an all day parking ticket and, as the weather was very pleasant, we took a rug and books etc. with us and went back onto the sand for our picnic. The dogs were quite tired and content to walk on their leads until we found the right spot at the foot of the dunes to erect the wind break and settle down for food and a snooze. They had a nap too, exhausted by their mad capers.

By mid-afternoon, David roused and strolled down to inspect the sea which was much nearer now. The decision to go in or not had to be made soon. He reported back that a few people were having a 'go', but that the waves were puny and they were all standing about waiting for the big one which did not come, and getting colder and colder in the process. After the excitement of the last few days we were tired so we decided not to venture into the water but to return instead to Rose-in-Vale and sit by the pool until it was time to change for dinner, maybe have a real swim if the water was warm.

Next morning we set off for Holywell bay. Any chance of a surf would be late afternoon, so the morning belonged to the dogs. There were lots of families camping round the back of the dunes out of the brisk wind off the sea. The little river describes a sinuous course around the dunes and is just the right size for paddling and damming, so this is a popular spot with children The boys were getting the hang of this holiday lark and were really naughty. They chased a Jack Russell into the river, which then fled back to its owners and shook river all over them, not a popular move! Next they rushed madly round the various encampments, panicking the children and thrusting black noses into snoozing faces. No amount of calling had any effect, so we hurried on, hoping they would be afraid to lose us and follow. They did and we rounded the corner into the wind. The beach is huge and we had a super walk, but we had to keep moving because the wind was strong and cold, in fact it had kept everyone else round the back of the dunes and we only shared the acres of sand with one other dog walker. After about an hour we bribed them back to us with a biscuit and put leads on, before running the gauntlet of the picnickers again. The surf had looked really promising and we were anxious to get back to Perran in time to catch the tide at its peak. We parked in the beach park as usual and began the business of getting out of our clothes and into swimsuits and wet suits. We achieved this in the front seats of the car, both for reasons of modesty and for warmth. In the late September breeze people passing were huddled into anoraks, sweaters and head scarves, which adds to the incredulity with which we are surreptitiously observed, gyrating and grunting in the shelter of the car doors as we struggle into our gear.

A wet suit to be effective has to fit like an all over roll-on corset, and getting into and out of it is as energetic as the actual bathe. It is also a hilarious spectator sport when indulged in by two grey-haired wrinklies! The youngsters make no trouble of it at all, as their strong young arms haul the leggings up their muscular legs and reach over to find with ease the top to pull up the zip which runs from hips to neck at the back. It is not quite the same with us. The suit fights not to be pulled up, it clings to flabby legs and refuses to engulf wobbly bottoms. Hands are not as strong as they were and, when you finally get the garment over your hips, you still have to force your arms through elastic tunnels (sleeves) a by repeated shoulder shrugging movements with luck your hands finally emerge to struggle a bit more to make the back zip meet. We then zip up each other. Bingo, now we look and walk like colourful penguins.

As the temperature was not likely to cause them any discomfort, we left the dogs in the car with all the windows and the roof open a few inches, before we waddled off to the fairly distant sea with our boards under our arms. These days belly boards are moulded sledge-shaped things, with leashes like the real thing. Ours date back to

David's childhood when his father actually had them made. They are about 4'6" long by 12" wide with a slight upward curve at the front end, and if the wind is strong they act as a sail as you cross the sand. The permitted bathing area is marked by two flags and patrolled by a hunky Australian lifeguard sitting in a special 'beach buggy', with his surf board at the ready to launch into the waves to rescue any foolish bathers who get into difficulties. He also has a loud hailer so that if any of his flock stray outside the flagged limits they are quickly brought to heel again. There are usually two or more doting females hanging around, hypnotised by this splendid specimen of manhood, but he is ignoring them steadfastly while he is on duty, undoubtedly their devotion will be rewarded later!

We shed our flip-flops and got into the water. I am always apprehensive of our first dip; after another year will we still be able to do it? Or will the strength of the swell beat us? Do we in fact look ridiculous to the other folk on the beach? Do we care? "No". Will the water be perishing in spite of our wet suits? "Yes," but after just one run the old thrill is there; the adrenaline surges and we stay in until we are exhausted. Before wet suit days we had to come out because we were frozen, so they are certainly worth the struggle to get into them. The other surfers look at our antique boards in disbelief, until they see us catching waves and zooming further up the beach than they are. It is a most exhilarating sport and it is like riding a bicycle, once you have the knack it is easy. When we have had enough our wet suits make the walk back more comfortable as they continue to keep us warm, no need for towels to huddle into.

We got back to the car having run the gauntlet of anorak clad folk watching us with undisguised interest, obviously considering us quite mad. Although there are a few other surfers they are all either children or athletic young men, so two OAP's tend to stand out! The dogs were very pleased to see us and we let them out of the car and tied their leads to a convenient seat, so that we could get changed without their help. Getting out of the wet suit is quicker than getting into it but just as much fun for passers by. We each helped the other, having first unzipped and freed our arms. I sat on the tail gate first and hung on while David pulled the empty arms off, then peeled me like a banana skin until I popped out and catapulted back into the boot. Shivering in just my swimsuit, I then peeled him, and we quickly shut ourselves into the car, out of the wind, to dry and dress hampered by cold fingers and sticky, salty bodies. Clammy flesh resisted knickers which rolled up in protest at being hauled up damp legs and over cold bottoms in the confined space but we got there and clutched a welcome cup of coffee at last.

All the time we are performing, so are the boys. They tried hard to tow the bench towards us, but when that defeated them they got their leads in such a tangle that they finished trussed up like a couple of chickens. A dog lover tapped the car window just as I was trying to haul my jeans up over my tacky legs with my numb fingers and he insisted that they were strangling themselves. David was getting on better than I was and he got out to investigate. They were just in front of the car in fact but a litter bin blocked our view. They were pleased to be released and jumped back into the car with alacrity.

Robert, Rachael and James were also in Cornwall. The boys are so keen on Malibu surfing that they often drive three hundred odd miles to spend a long weekend near Newquay. In a caravan by night and in the sea by day. This year Rachael's birthday fell due while they were down here and, to celebrate, we invited them to dinner at our hotel. It was a double celebration as James had just received his certificate, the proof that at last he is a fully fledged solicitor. We explained the reasons for our celebrations to our hotelier, Mr Arthur, and we were given a superb meal. A very good time was had by all except the dogs, who had to spend the evening from 8.00 p.m. imprisoned in the car. We reminisced about the holidays we had spent all together, coming back year after year to a caravan at Treyarnon and their first attempts at surfing. Being dutiful parents we sat on the cliffs for hours, watching their efforts to get perpendicular on their boards. As the maximum time they achieved upright was thirty seconds before they fell off it was very hard to get a photographic record of the magic moment, as no one had a video camera in those days!

It was almost 11.00 p.m. before we said goodbye to them and hurried out to rescue Tom and Gill. They had shredded the old car rug which we had draped over the back seat to protect it, alas no more. They forgot their frustration as soon as they saw us however, and went wild with excitement at the prospect of their evening walk. It was a very energetic one, for we went up the narrow lane opposite the gates as the high banks and tall trees on both sides made an inky tunnel and they pulled us from side to side as they caught one exciting scent after another. We let them have their fun, although it was quite exciting for us being towed to and fro and not being able to see a thing in the blackness. We somehow kept our feet and emerged at the top to see a clear sky and stars; what stars! Not like any stars we see near home, where all-night street lights and the smoggy atmosphere leave only the brightest still visible. Here the sky is full of stars, the Milky Way, the Seven Sisters, the Bull and Cassiopeia, the memories came flooding back from my childhood days, when, as a girl guide, I was earning my astronomer's badge. We found the Plough and followed the line of the last two stars up to the Pole star, the last and brightest star in the Little Bear's tail. When we reached the top of the hill we could see the Southern hemisphere too, and there was Orion with his belt and sword. The hill is steep and the extra energy we expended by following the zigzagging dogs made us puff, so we were glad to linger awhile at this vantage point, absorbing the beauty of the sky and listening to the sounds of the night - no cars - just an owl calling somewhere and the wind in the trees. A satisfying end to a super day.

We slept well and so did the boys, with their heads on their ridiculous blankets on the floor beside our bed. The call of nature forced me to get out at around 6.00a.m and, forgetting all about them, I walked on a leg, but I only got my foot kicked, no hard feelings, not even a squeak!

What a surprise! Today we bumped into Rolf Harris at the Lost Gardens of Heligan. We were intrigued by the description of the project which was to rescue the completely over grown gardens from their counterpane of ivy, brambles and other thugs and when we read that dogs on leads were welcome, off we went. We were waiting at the entrance to pay when a young lady asked us about the dogs, "We've got one like that at home" she said. We were swapping stories about them when up strolled Rolf Harris - her Dad! I have been a fan of his ever since the children and I glued ourselves to Blue Peter to watch him produce huge paintings in a matter of seconds. Wielding a distemper brush he created scene after scene. I can still remember being fascinated as he captured the paint as it ran down and redirected it to become another part of the picture. He would always finish with a few dabs of black then white, still using a huge brush, and just touching the paper with the tips of the bristles. Suddenly the whole painting would come to life. What a talent! The times I tried to copy him, on a smaller scale I hasten to add! Anyway he too had fallen under the spell of a big Poodle. We chatted for quite a time about our holy terrors and all agreed that dogs will be dogs, but Poodles are something else!

Chapter 11

WE DO LIKE TO BE BESIDE THE SEASIDE

The next day was very windy and heavy black clouds chased across the sky, endlessly trying to catch one another other up. The sun shone briefly in between showers but it was not winning. As it was too chilly to sit about we drove south to Portreath where the bakery shop is famous for its pasties and gorgeous cream cakes but as "sorry no dogs" greeted us on the beach we went on to Godrevy Point, a lonely National Trust area. That was 'no dogs' too, but as there were no people there either, we decided to stay and ignore the sign. After a walk we returned to the car, with good appetites for the pasties - the best in the south west - they were too! Pasties can be very dodgy. They all look golden and delicious, like the ones we had today, but we have sampled almost inedible specimens with cardboard coats and India rubber insides which looked just as appetising. It is worth a detour to a good pasty shop once you have found one.

We were sitting in the car munching away. We had the windows open and were enjoying the view of the rugged cliffs and pounding sea, when a large dilapidated van drew up just near by. Our eyes were naturally drawn towards it, and stayed there! It was driven by a hippie girl of indeterminate age and was obviously her home. The dashboard was decorated with cacti in pots sequinned dolls, and curtains. We could not help wondering what happened if she braked suddenly, especially to the cacti! After a moment or two, she emerged. A pair of Doc. Martins appeared below the driving door, followed by red cotton striped trousers which were topped (we could now see the whole vision) by three shirts, all different lengths and colours and all worn outside the trousers. On top of all this, and shortest of all, was a black sweater. Her head was swathed in a red scarf almost hiding her long hair. We watched fascinated. She seemed to be alone. She never once glanced in our direction; she just sat on a rock with her back to us and munched an apple. She looked sad and lonely and we felt ashamed of our curiosity and left her to her solitude.

We needed to do some shopping so, we drove to Perran, parked, and instead of shutting them in the car again we put their leads on and took them with us. The busy main street is just behind the beach and lots of the shops overflow onto the pavement, displaying rails of lurid tee-shirts, racks of buckets, spades, beach shoes etc. All the clutter you would find in any sea side town. For the boys it was a new experience, an adventure no less, but we kept them on very short leads fearing the quick cocking of a leg over a display of beach wear, or worse, up a greengrocery stand! Vigilance paid and we completed the excursion without any impromptu christenings. We took turns to hold them, while the interested party went into the shop. They sat like angels and were fussed and petted by endless passers by who were fooled into thinking what good boys they were!

David, who has very fair skin, bought three cotton beach hats, one blue, one beige and one white. I pointed out that he was practically guaranteeing that we got no sun at all but he said he would wear them at home anyway and he could not get them in Luton. I conceded defeat, as it was certainly better than the knotted hankie I have known him resort to in the past!

It is Saturday already, the holiday flying as usual. We were near Chapel Porth and that is where we headed for a romp and a paddle. It is a very beautiful Nature Trust owned bay, with high rocky cliffs on both sides and dunes at the back. It was so pleasant out of the wind in the dunes that we made a nest and stayed there, watching the sea. The boys roamed around happily. We had plenty to watch as there was a surfing competition taking place. The contestants wore colourful wet suits with even more colourful boards, which made them very visible as they soared up and down the faces of the racing waves looking as if they were glued to their boards as if gravity did not exist.

He's gone to sleep - let's explore.

Doesn't it taste funny?

I can smell rabbits.

Further along the beach the lifeguards were on duty for the benefit of folk like us and we decided to stay and have our dip. We shut the dogs in the car, with windows open, of course and had a really exciting surf, the current strong and the waves fierce, though if we had not made our minds up to go in when we did we would have missed our chance because, just as we were thinking that we had had nearly enough, the life guards whistled us out and put up the red flag, which is the no bathing signal used when conditions are dangerous. No wonder we enjoyed it! The dogs were rested and raring to go again, so when we were dressed we took them back to the beach for a further romp. They chased sea gulls and discovered what fun rock climbing is, giving us a few more grey hairs, then a German Shepherd with a ball caught their attention and Tom chased the ball into a rock pool and found himself out of his depth and swimming for the first time. Gill preferred to watch. His body language said it all "It is bad enough when 'they' bath us, swimming for fun is not our scene".

Propped up against rock, an elderly couple were relaxing and watching the world go by when the pair found an absolutely marvellous smell, which required extensive excavation beside, and practically underneath, the spot where they were sitting. In a flash there was sand flying everywhere, so we hastened to the rescue and hauled them off, apologising as usual. They were friendly folk and thought it was quite funny, thank goodness. We kept them on leads until we thought they had forgotten - when will we learn? The second we let them go they raced back and resumed digging. Even more embarrassed, we hurried back and once again removed them, with much tugging and back peddling on their part, so they then stayed on their leads back to the car! The victims actually thought they were lovely - yuck, why does everybody think they are cute dogs, they should try living with them!

We have been away from home for nearly a week now and the car is beginning to look and smell like a stable. The dog food which has fallen into the groves round the boot lid is going green and furry. There is sand everywhere. The door pockets have been raided and there are paw-prints all over the dash-board. The back seat contents have been trampled and thoroughly searched for edibles and all the windows have been steamed up and dribbled down. Crumbs from the picnic basket lurk deep in the cracks between the seat cushions and seat belt buckles. The whole thing is quite revolting. How now we regret not fixing a secure dog guard before we came! We have plenty of time to notice the smell and the reasons for it today, as it is teeming with rain and we are marooned inside. If it does not improve within an hour we shall have to kit up and sally forth regardless, then we can add wet dog to the other smells!

It did stop eventually and we went on our usual walk to the end of Perran beach and back, trying as we went to teach them to retrieve a ball. Tom was beginning to get the idea when they were distracted by three Labradors who were so friendly that Tom and Gill decided to go back to the cliff top caravan site with them up a long steep zig-zag stairway, but thank goodness, when they realised we were not following they hurtled back down to us and we quickly put their leads on, as we had spotted three ponies approaching along the sea edge. We were not sure whether Tom still remembered 'Evil' and we did not trust them not to go over and either scare the ponies enough to make them bolt, endangering their young riders, or get injured if the ponies kicked out at them. They were very cross and pulled like mad, but we hung onto them until the ponies were a good half a mile away and we thought it was safe - wrong - they both set off instantly like greyhounds following the scent of the hoof prints in the sand until they were just black dots. Luckily they rely entirely on their noses and completely missed the horses who had decided to have a paddle at just the right moment. After they lost the scent they searched around for a bit and then raced back to us. This time we put leads on to stay on!

Ahead of us there was a small crowd of people watching something near Chapel Rock in the centre of the beach at the town end. Curiosity drew us to the spot too. It was the swimming leg of a triathlon race. There were at least thirty competitors and in the choppy rough sea we did not envy them. They had to swim out to a special marker bouy and back, it looked miles. Several of them did not make it, so were brought back exhausted in the rescue boat, victims of the rough sea and strong currents. The ones that did make it ran back up the beach to start the cycle race. To think they do it for fun!

There are always one or two adult beach toys that are new to us and, as we turned back from the sea and started to walk back to the car, our attention was taken by a go-cart whizzing along, towed by a maggot-shaped kite in the sky way above. It looked huge fun, but as we watched there was a momentary lull in the wind, the kite plummeted down and, although we watched several abortive attempts to re-launch it, they were in vain and when eventually it was air-borne it was only about two minutes before it scythed to earth again. A very stop-go pastime, we felt.

When the next day, Monday, turned out wet again we decided to have a major shopping day. First, kitted out in our waterproofs we gave the boys a beach run and then took off in the direction of Liskeard to a huge trading estate we discovered years ago. It is called Trago Mills and there are such bargains to be had that we had come armed with a shopping list for the DIY and garden department. After about a couple of hours we had bought chicken wire netting, mixed bulbs, new dog collars, a blue track suit for me and some presents to take home. The rain hit us like a car wash as we emerged, so once again lunch was a pasty consumed in the car, with the boys helping with leftovers.

Our favourite part of Cornwall is the Trevose peninsular. It has a series of fabulous bays which face the Atlantic and often get cracking surf. On the other sheltered side is the estuary of the river Camel and Padstow, which provides a total contrast, with its quaint narrow streets and busy harbour. It is just the place to do some shopping for gifts to take home or to buy fresh prawn sandwiches for lunch. If we decide to stay and explore Padstow, we can take a boat trip to catch mackerel or see the sea birds, Puffin island being the usual trip, or go across the estuary on the little ferry to Rock, where the sandy shores are for sunbathing or a gentle swim if the sun does change its mind and smile on us.

The fishy smells, the coils of rope and lobster pots lead you along the quay to see the live lobsters in huge holding tanks of salt water, rather sad when you reflect on their fate. Hidden away up the steep back alleys of the town, are more shops, with gem-stone jewellery being made while you watch, or appetising aromas from little bakeries plus a super leather shop called Bag End that is no longer hidden in the back streets but has progressed to a prominent position nearer the harbour and always merits a visit. It smells deliciously of leather and they will put a buckle on a belt of your choice or make you a belt if none of the super designs tempts you; similarly if brooches, hair ornaments or bracelets are your choice they are all there. In spite of the shell shops and gifts shops the town is not as spoilt as some of the other similar Cornish towns. Maybe because it is also still a busy working harbour servicing the fishing vessels, the tourists are more of a summer diversion.

We decided to do a detour to this area, and if we were lucky, have a surf. The town centre of Wadebridge is the cause of a constant bottle neck, but we got through eventually and headed straight for Treyanon. The weather relented, the skies still threatened but the rain stopped. We parked by the caravan site as we have done so many times over the years. The rain had sent the car park man home early so we were £1 better off! We took the boys on leads along the cliff tops towards Constantine, the next bay; as we walked we watched the waves breaking on the rocks as they have been doing for thousands of years, the spray hurled high into the air, spreading foam across the grass. Great booming sounds echoed up from a spot called the blow hole, where the rocks have been worn away to form a smooth basin with a chimney up through a cleft in the cliff, spray pumping out of this vent with every fresh wave. At this stage of the tide it is quite spectacular when the sea is rough.

There were lots of other canine walkers and the dogs enjoyed themselves off their leads until they took exception to a noisy Jack Russell and chased it out of sight. The owner was very put out and, when I attempted to apologise, I got the "these dogs should be on lead" reaction. The fact that his dog started it was overlooked! When we reached Constantine beach we tried the ball retrieving game again, but Gill spoilt it all the time by running off and dropping it when we were not looking, causing a hold up while we searched for it. The surf was getting better and better and we soon decided that the dogs had had their turn and it was now ours. We hurried back to the car, gave them a chew each, and struggled into our wet suits. The sea was terrific, huge waves gave us splendid runs and sent us back for more until we were exhausted. It was to prove the best surf of the holiday.

When we returned really tired to the car, it was to discover Gill with his mouth full of bread roll - the last bread roll. One or other black nose had managed to force the zip on the picnic bag. They preferred our picnic to their chews, they said. The twenty five miles back to Rose-in-Vale seemed endless because we were so exhausted, and when we did get back we had both stiffened up so much we could hardly get out of the car! Never mind, it was worth it and it is wonderful what a hot bath and a large sherry can do!

When we return from a hard day's pleasure walking and swimming, the first thing on the agenda is doggy tea, partaken on a large plastic mat in our tiny bathroom. At the same time we run the first bath. They are very interested in this and hang their heads over to test the foam or give a protruding knee a helpful lick. One night we forgot to refill their water bowl and Tom was so thirsty from all the salt water that he tried hard to drink my very hot foamy bath water until the penny dropped and I shouted to David to give them a refill. This was noisily and untidily absorbed and a meaningful look meant another refill was needed before their thirst was quenched and they could turn their attention to their food. They are so good natured; another night Tom was once again on bath duty and though I reached for the towel with my eyes shut and stuck my questing fingers in his face, he still stayed to monitor my ablutions to make sure I made as good a job of mine, as I did of his on bath day.

The return to a dark, chilly car while we had our dinner was not popular, but the final stroll up the lane and back was joyfully anticipated. They could not contain their excitement and barked to the night that they were coming. We were extraordinarily lucky weather wise on these nocturnal excursions and it seemed that most nights we were lit by the moon and stars, which made the tree tunnel seem like black velvet, so dark that you could imagine you had your eyes closed. We had to keep them on leads or they would have been away in pursuit of some creature or other, and black dogs are not the easiest thing to find on a dark night! However, this made the walk very energetic for us. We had to keep up with them as they

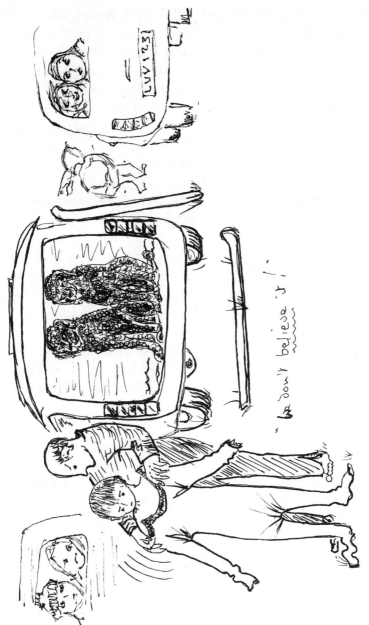

Getting ready for the briney.

found one scent after another and tried to dive into the hedge in pursuit. I am sure my arms are longer than they were! Most nights we heard the tawny owl, and we had a big thrill one night when we actually saw him sitting on a telegraph pole, silhouetted against the sky. We thought of the other guests still in the bar, and were glad we were "us."

After our fantastic surf yesterday we decided to return to Treyanon. It was drizzling when we arrived so once again we ate our picnic in the car, with steamy fog created by four damp bodies clouding up the windows. When we emerged our attention was taken by a mauve Mini that was being driven down the steep slip-way and onto the soft sand above the tide line. We both thought it must be driven by crazy teenagers, it was so obvious that it would get stuck! We watched, fascinated, as he attempted to circle back having realised his folly. It ground to a halt facing the slip-way about twenty yards away. Panic set in and, with the engine revving furiously, and the wheels spinning, it was soon up to its axles and still digging in! We began to feel sorry for the driver, who ever it was; then he or she gave up and switched off the engine. What a surprise we had! It was a large elderly lady who emerged! There was nobody about so we went over to offer help. As we approached another large lady go out from the other side. We could hardly believe our eyes. They just wanted to turn round, they said. In fact they had just passed the wide entrance to the parking field where they could have turned with ease! It was obvious that a tow was the only way out, we suggested that a farmer on a tractor who was visible just a field away, might be persuaded to help. They did not want to know! They belonged to the AA and they were going to phone from a nearby hotel. There was nothing more we could do, it had stopped raining so we took the dogs for a run along the cliffs.

When we eventually sauntered back, two hours later, they were still there, from the cliff top we could also see a yellow van approaching. Their knight in shining armour, no less. We would love to have read his thoughts when saw the pickle they were in! I bet he will tell the tale a few times to his friends in the pub. He spoke to the hapless pair and then went off to enlist the help of the farmer who was still busy ploughing.

We settled down to watch from our vantage point on the cliffs. The AA man returned with the farmer (and his tractor). He turned the damsels in distress out onto the sand and took the wheel himself. There was a minor problem when the chain was too short but another piece was added and the farmer gently took the strain in. At first the tractor skidded, the gradient was steep and covered in wind blown sand, but then he got a grip and slowly the little car emerged from its hole and crept to the slip-way on the end of the chain. The chain was removed and the engine started. In the capable hands of the knight it mounted the slope to safety. He did not take any chances with the owner; he did not hand it over until he had it turned round for her. Who knows, the geriatric Sterling Moss might have put it in reverse and landed back on the sand again!

Chapter 12

FUN ON THE FARM

When the family were young we came to Cornwall every year and for many of those first years we stayed on a farm near Camelford. We are still friends with the farmer and his wife nearly thirty years later. We pop in unannounced each year and swap our family news over a cuppa in the kitchen. Since we saw them last year they have retired and moved to a bungalow in Devon. We phoned their son Richard for directions and, after saying goodbye to Tony and Vanda at the hotel for another year, we set off to find them on our way home.

My first taste of Cornwall was when I was twenty and mad enough to bounce all the way down the A303 on the back of my boyfriend's 350 CC Royal Enfield to join his family for two weeks in Perranporth. We were in love and bathed in that magic glow that envelops lovers and Cornwall became part of it. The rugged north coast, with the awe inspiring sea (my family used to go to Frinton!) became a Mecca for us. The spectacular scenery, golden sands and surf pulled us back to spend our honeymoon at Newquay and from then to return almost every year for over forty years to date.

The memories crowd in on us as we drive along the familiar roads, lined with hedgerows pruned and tortured by the salt laden westerly gales into curious wedge shaped curves leaning over the road; some like huge hedgehogs, their outside twigs scorched and brown, survive by hiding their new growth under their dead umbrellas. The Scots pines on the hill tops are like giant bonsai on the sky line. In the valleys by contrast the trees stand tall and straight and the road runs through green tunnels, pruned this time by passing lorries and farm carts which leave hay as evidence of their passage as they dawdle along with mountainous loads of their sweet cargo. The farm was hidden down just such a lane. It was a real farm, an old fashioned one where the cows fed their own calves and the chickens and geese were everywhere. Under foot it was MUD, so wellies were needed every day - the children were in heaven as they 'helped' to feed the pigs and hens and to burrow in the nearly empty hay barn looking for eggs. It was in the early hours of one morning when our farmer friend woke us. We knew that a calf was going to arrive very soon and he asked if the children would like to see the birth. We thought it a splendid idea, a live biology lesson! It was on the point of arrival. Everyone was quickly dressed in sweaters and wellies and with excitement mounting we all trooped over to the barn. Robyn was twelve, Robert ten, James six and Joanne four; they would not forget this lesson.

It was magical to see the new baby emerge, helped by a heave from the farmer, and then watch it struggle to its feet in minutes after arriving. Its legs were all wobbly and spread out as it tried to balance in the straw. Its mother licked it clean and we left them both to return to our beds, very moved by what we had seen. An everyday event for a dairy farmer but an unforgettable experience for all of us. The children loved the farm so much that they almost forgot the 'sea-side' in their importance as farm workers. There were horses to ride just down the lane and riding lessons of a fairly basic nature were available. We all took advantage of this and, although at the end our riding skills were still minimal, we learned enough to have a super riding holiday later on. A source of fascination on the horse farm was an ancient privy at the bottom of the garden. It spanned a tiny stream - the user could be sitting there and a duck could swim in one side and out of the other. We assured the children it was not actually used anymore! The stream grew splendid watercress!

Enough reminiscing, we had to find our friends' new home. We drove along lanes whose stone wall 'hedges' were like endless gardens. Thrift, sea campion, pink campion, cow parsley, ferns, even a late foxglove or two grew out of them, a reminder of how much rain Cornwall has, even in a good summer. We stopped briefly for the boys' benefit as we did not want any accidents! The Devon bungalow was hidden away and took several more stops for directions before we eventually found it. They were delighted to see us, surprised and pleased that we had wanted to find them. Tom and Gill were viewed through the car windows and, although obviously daunted by their size, Suzanne bravely insisted that they came in with us. We grabbed a collar each and, once inside, shut the porch door firmly before letting go. Oh dear, they had run out of virtue for today and rushed into the adjoining kitchen, heading straight for the cat's dinner. In the rush the bowl was broken and the cat put to flight. Not a good start! Leads were put on and we offered to put them back in the car. Not a bit of it, Suzanne insisted that they stayed to meet Geoff, who at this stage was somewhere outside, tending his house cows. They settled down and looked sorry for their misdemeanour. As usual they won after a few remarks like "they are good really, just like black lambs" - "are they only ten months?"- "still puppies really". They soon had us fooled into letting them go again. It was a good thing that it was Suzanne who insisted, because it was she who had forgotten the bucket of full jersey cream milk, still warm, that was on the floor. They had a delicious long drink before we heard a slurping noise and went to see!!! By this time Geoffrey had come in and was sitting in the lounge chatting to David. I followed Suzanne out to the kitchen to put the kettle on and there they were, two black faces with white muzzles. She put her finger to her lips before I could shout at them "Don't tell Geoffrey" she said "he always boils it anyway"!

After about an hour catching up on our various news we made a move to leave, as we had a long ride ahead. I was saying a few final goodbyes to them both as they stood together in the kitchen. David was ahead with Tom, and Gill was at full stretch of my arm, with his lead round the corner in the porch, invisible from our angle, which was just as well as he had started to pee up the lovely smelly warehouse coat that Geoff had hung behind the door when he came in from the cow shed ! I stopped him almost in time!! We breathed a sigh of relief when we had them back in the car out of any more mischief and, with final waves, we departed homewards.

118

The Somerset countryside was enchanting as we drove along. Lovely wooded valleys and pretty villages bathed in sunshine. It was not to last. We soon noticed an ominous grey blanket ahead and quite suddenly the sun was switched off like a light and we ran into rain, which very rapidly became a deluge. This continued all the way to Hadspen House where I had eagerly anticipated a very special garden visit. This is reputed to be a superbly planted, colour co-ordinated gem of a place. I was not going to be cheated; the rain was still bucketing down when we got there but I donned full waterproofs and, leaving all the boys in the car, paid my entrance fee and bravely set out. Needless to say I was alone, no other idiots at all, and even I was forced to retreat to the potting shed after about a quarter of an hour of monsoon type rain. The genius behind the planting schemes, Nori Pope was busy potting up cuttings and very happy to talk to another gardening addict. I never did see the whole garden, but what I did see, even in those conditions, made me determined to return another year. Before I left I asked where we could give the dogs a stretch and he directed us on, up their muddy lane to a huge stubble field. We parked in the gateway and ate our lunch, by which time the rain had eased somewhat. As I was soaked already, I offered to do a circuit of the field with the dogs while David had a snooze - another snooze!

We had actually felt a little apprehensive about leaving the car in its isolated spot with all our luggage and holiday gear inside. We had noticed a gypsy encampment not far back down a side turning. We could be in trouble! We played safe and I squelched forth on my own again. Every furrow was a pond, so in seconds the boys were soaked and filthy. I reflected that this clay mud was not going to shake off their coats and we were going to have fun getting them into any sort of decent state to be received into some unsuspecting guest house in a few hours time! The field was huge and featureless; it dipped away from the car, which was soon out of sight. Without actually counting I remember going round four corners and was expecting to see the car at any moment, but there was no sign of it. After a longish walk through sticky mud, stumbling in and out of ruts I was tired and fed up. I arrived at gate number five, still no car. I had a moment of mild panic, had I missed it? Should I go back? The boys were still tearing about, mud up to their armpits and under their bellies, so they, at least, were enjoying themselves. I paused, I was sure I had not missed a car, I couldn't have, and goodness knows I was anxious enough to get back inside it. I pressed on and in about a hundred yards, there thank heaven was another gate, and the car at last. The rain had waited until I was at the furthest point from base before it started again; this time ominous rumbles of thunder accompanied it. I was so glad to be back that trying to clean the boys up under the shelter of the tail-gate did not seem too bad after all. It was raining so hard that much of the mud had washed off and I threw the wet towels in with them to absorb a bit more, before I turned my attention to myself. Like an idiot I had taken my water proof trousers off after my garden trip and, as it had stopped raining at the start of the walk, I had not put them on again. My top was dry under my jacket but the wet had crept up my trousers from the run off and my thighs were soaked. I finished up sitting on a newspaper with another on my lap to try and soak up some of the water. We had the heater on and the windows shut in an attempt to dry off. It was like a sauna and visibility was down to the span of the wipers. The thunder got closer, the rain got even heavier. The humidity in the car was so high we practically had clouds forming round our heads!

Every dip in the road was under water. It got worse and worse, with flooding and diversions becoming more and more frequent. We were having to turn back or get stuck and the nearer we got to Bath the worse it became. Although it was only 3.30 in the afternoon it was dark already. We decided that in our sodden state it would be very antisocial to arrive anywhere but home, even supposing we could actually find a way of getting to our destination without swimming! Accordingly we stopped in the next village, found a phone and explained our predicament. The proposed B and B actually adjoined a small river which had almost burst its banks already and they seemed relieved to hear from me that we were not coming - they had problems enough! A look at the map showed us that we were only a few miles from the M4 and a straight route home. It was a slow crawl to get there, however, with more floods to negotiate but we were lucky; we passed several stranded cars, but we got safely home at last.

The dogs were ecstatic to be back; the cats on the other hand had decided that the beastly black things had gone for ever and it was back to the good old days. They were rudely awoken from their sleep on the boiler and hopped hastily up to the top of the cupboard, from which haven they swore profusely at their enemies who were busy polishing off their tea, having stood on their hind legs and daintily lifted the bowls from the draining board to the floor. It tasted wonderful, especially as it was forbidden fruit. I shouted at them too late and shooed them outside, where they rushed about, noses to the ground, checking on all the strangers who had visited in their absence. Very elderly bones were re-discovered (yuck) and gnawed with relish.

David started emptying the car and was soon calling for help. No wonder, it was in a disgusting mess. There was dog food in an advanced state of decay in all the crevices, plus sand, bits of chewed wood from the beach, and shredded tissues. There is something about tissues, paper towels or 'J' cloths which fascinates them. They settle down with the prize between their paws and very delicately shred it into tiny pieces, at which point having made the maximum amount of mess they abandon the game. Once the boot was restored to its normal, bearably grotty state, we turned our attention to the back seat. The cushions and door panels had to be scrubbed thanks to the butter episode; the gaps were packed with crushed biscuit and fluff and it took most of the morning, but we were pleased with our efforts. The door pockets and the dashboard cubby hole were de-gritted with the vacuum and the instrument panel and windows were cleaned - it was a different car, we could almost sell it!

Chapter 13

WEEKS TO FORGET

The cats are messy eaters; they remove each piece of food from the dish to the floor before eating or rejecting it! David stood on a lump of clotted sheep's blood deemed inedible by one or other of the darlings. It stuck to his shoe. He then trod blood all over the hall, bedroom and bathroom. He only realised what he had done when it stuck to the white loo mat. He was suitably contrite, but if he had taken his stroll over the new carpet he might not have lived to tell the tale!

It is Monday - I hate Mondays. I found the washing machine had stuck halfway through its program, full of suddy clothes and dirty water. That was only the beginning as Tabatha had been sick on the new stair carpet. As a result I was late for work, and spent all morning trying to catch up. I made myself even later by repeating the account of my bad start to each patient in turn, to excuse my lateness. They seemed it highly entertaining but I was not amused because knew what awaited me at home. When I did get back, very late of course, it was to find that someone had eaten one of my new Clark's shoes. The probable sinner was Gill. After a hasty lunch I tackled the load of soggy clothes. Washing machines are wonderful when they work. When they don't you are stuck without any aids at all - no spin dryer or Granny's mangle, just person power. I finished at last, hanging out the clothes to drip, then mopping the large pool on the floor.

By bed time I was shattered and acting like a zombie. My last chore was to feed the cats - I wish I hadn't because in my fuddled state I put the half tin back in the fridge - upside down! Poor David nearly ruptured himself trying not to laugh. There was Whiskas dripping through the shelves, onto the bottom of the fridge and then onto the floor. The dogs cleaned the floor and offered to attend to the fridge too,but I declined. Then I saw the funny side too and we both collapsed laughing before staggering to bed still giggling.

The very next day I arrived home to find that someone had chewed the hall rug. I am sure it is Gill although why he has started to do it I have no idea.

One day when I was looking at a rack of leads, muzzles, brushes, clippers etc., I spotted the Haltis. I had once heard someone recommend them and am willing to try any thing! Haltis are as the name suggests, similar to a halter with one strap round the neck and another round the nose, side pieces connecting the two. The secret of control is that the nose band is threaded through a ring under the chin and when the lead is pulled taut the nose strap tightens, pulls the dog's mouth shut and his nose down - he hates this and soon learns that if he stops pulling it slackens immediately! At frequent intervals during the first half mile Gill pranced about shaking his head, going backwards and sideways to try to get rid of the nasty thing. Each time gentle tension on the lead sorted him out. A miracle had happened, he was walking beside me with his lead slack. Why hasn't someone told me how wonderful they are before this?

The white tomcat who lives along our route is a super cat and regards dogs as being quite beneath his notice - regardless of their size. He is a pain; the dogs know where he lives and get all keyed up as we approach. I scan doorsteps and window sills to try and spot him first to gain an advantage. He was there, sunbathing on the pavement just ahead and it was quite obvious that he was not going to move! He stayed put so I practically lifted them off their feet, the Haltis rendering them helpless and speechless, and we all crossed the road - on six legs - two each! A man cleaning his car watched with interest but did not shoo the cat away, perhaps he was looking forward to a bust up - if so he was disappointed! Mercifully the cat had gone when we came back..

I wish I could forget today. If only one could put the clock back and start again. As it was Tuesday I was on my own and as usual I took them to the park. Although I had them under control in their Haltis they were very excited ; we seemed to see even more cats than normal, in doorways, on steps, or just strolling in the road ahead, and I was very glad when we reached the park and I could safely release them - or so I thought. I let them go and walked along the familiar path, swinging their leads, not a care in the world. They vanished, but that is nothing unusual, they tear ahead hoping to catch a squirrel unawares (no chance) and I assumed that was what they were up to. Then I heard someone screaming from a nearby garden. They had found a gap in the fence, squeezed through it and were chasing a pet rabbit. Before I had really taken in the situation, Gill had caught it and was back through the fence, and away. How was he to know that this rabbit was different to the ones he regularly chased up at the airport. I sprinted after him but it was too late - he had killed it. He dropped it and fled ; he knew from the panic in my voice that he was in trouble and was soon a blob in the distance.

The distraught woman, whose pet it was, ran after me, still screaming. We found the lifeless body and I attempted to comfort her, but she was naturally hysterical. Tom and Gill were running round even more hyped up by all the noise. There was quite an audience by then and I decided the best thing to do was to take the dogs home. I called to the woman that I would come back and, having captured them both, I left the scene as fast as I could. I did not shout at them; how could they be expected to know the difference between one rabbit and another. Once I was home I shut them in the house and drove back. I was extremely upset myself; to lose a beloved pet in such a horrible way was terrible ; I dreaded facing her.

I found her in the garden. I tried to say how sincerely sorry I was. I said that they had never harmed anything before, but chasing rabbits was to them just doing what comes naturally. She refused to let me buy a replacement. I had to offer, although I knew what a poor substitute it was; we were both in tears. She said that her two young sons would be home from school in a few minutes and what could she tell them? I felt like the lowest form of pond life and slunk miserably home. The dogs were waiting for me, quite unaware of

We'll teach you, "So what"!

their crime and mystified by my emotion. I made a cup of tea and swallowed a couple of aspirins, my head throbbing. I had hardly poured it into the cup when the door bell rang and there stood the council dog warden. She came in and met them, seeing for herself that they were not the vicious killers her informant had described, but just friendly family pets.

I explained that the hunting instinct was in their genes and they regularly followed rabbit tracks and dug fruitlessly at burrows on our wilder walks. They had never been aggressive to cats, in fact we had three of our own. I even told her of our efforts to prevent them becoming sheep chasers when we got the farmer to pen them with a ram in order to teach them a painful lesson. She was understanding of our problems. She knew that with their breed hunting is a dominant feature, but nevertheless from now on we must keep them under control the whole time we are in the park. This would make the whole walk pointless. It is very sad, as the park is so convenient and the squirrels have provided such good sport; we are going to have to go further afield from now on, that at least is certain. It also means that they will only get a walk when we can both take them. I am not big and strong enough to handle them on my own if they decide to do their own thing.

David loves black pudding, and as it was a golf day he considered a cooked breakfast justifiable as he is sure he burns off the extra calories. My motto is anything for a quiet life, so a cooked breakfast it was to be! I found egg, bacon, sausage, mushrooms, tomatoes and his treat - the black pudding. I had just assembled everything when the postman rang the bell. I went to the door, took the bundle of mail and gave it a very brief scrutiny, before putting it on the table and returning to the kitchen. Of the black pudding there was no trace; on the floor was a rasher of bacon that had been sampled and discarded and Gill was leaving the scene of the crime in a hurry! I cooked what was left, having added more bacon, but there was no more black pudding, oh dear. At the table David watched his plate arrive with happy anticipation "where is my black pudding, I have been looking forward to that, I got it specially." Reply "in your black dog!" His answer - censored!

I was looking at the Saturday paper later that week and saw a picture of a dog and the caption "School for scoundrels". I read with growing interest of other doggy hooligans who drove their owners to their limits. I was gratified to see that some dogs were even worse than ours! One determined canine pulled over and then towed along his 17 stone owner! Are they sure it is a dog they have, not a donkey? The nub of the article was that, scattered throughout the land, there are patient, calm, determined people who manage to train these doggy delinquents at a kind of canine Borstal. Three addresses were given. A Cambridgeshire one was the nearest. We guessed it would be expensive but what joy to have two obedient dogs; if we arranged to send them there instead of kennels while we went away we should avoid a double expense, it would be more than worth it.

I was quite sure the phone would be jammed with other desperate dog owners seeking help having also read the article. At 9.15 a.m. I tried the number. A kind voice answered and apologised for keeping me waiting, his wife had to fetch him from the bottom kennels, he said. He listened to my tale of woe, "Standard poodles, three and a half year old litter brothers!" He considered their sins. I had said they are chasers, pullers and thieves. "If I had them for six weeks, (he sighed, £-signs flashed before my eyes), I could probably train them out of all their habits except chasing live game, as that is in their blood, but although they would behave for me, as soon they were home, like as not, they would remember the good old days, and BINGO all the boring new tricks would be forgotten and you would be much poorer and still in trouble - I am sorry !" What a lovely man! But we are left at square one. On their walk later that day, they behaved like angels - they had obviously been listening and did not fancy doggy holiday camp!

Chapter 14

"THE BEST LAID SCHEMES O'MICE AND MEN GANG AFT AGLEY AND LEA'E US NOUGHT BUT GRIEF AND PAIN FOR PROMISED JOY"

Robert Burns

Winston, my brother, and Elizabeth, my sister in law, live in Troon near Ayr. They are both very fond of animals, they have three Jack Russell terriers and two cats, but the temporary addition of two large Poodles was agreed to a trifle reluctantly, we thought, not surprising when you think of their size. Robert had visited with Max on a previous occasion and all had been well then, so full of optimism we started off laden as for Cornwall with doggie luggage as well as Christmas and birthday presents from all the family to every one in Scotland, as we were unlikely to see them again before the festivities.

We first drove to Popes Meadow for a run to settle them. They were delighted to be having a walk so early in the morning and were full of beans. As we rounded a corner, coming up the sports field towards us was a bull terrier with its owner. The pair bounded over to say 'hello' as usual but the stranger took fright and ran away back down the hill, with Tom in top gear behind him. Gill incredibly responded to our shouts and stopped, but Tom was having too much fun and chased the dog out of the park, straight across a very busy main road, into another part of the park where we never go because there is a lake, and lots of ducks - need I say more. We were helpless, he just vanished and we were a hundred yards away at least. He came back eventually, miraculously picking another gap in the traffic by sheer luck, as he just ran straight across again. We scolded him but were too relieved that he was safe to be very cross. The Bull Terrier's owner meanwhile had not even turned his head; he just kept walking up the hill and let his dog fend for itself!

walkies?

I can't see where I'm going.

Just before junction thirteen, fifteen miles or so up the M1, I suddenly remembered that the box of presents was still sitting at home. As well as Christmas presents there were lots of garden plants and two huge bunches of nerine lilies, one for Elizabeth and one for Mother. We had to go back. We were rather quiet in the car, we had not made a very good start one way and another!

After the long journey, with just two stops for a picnic and a "wee" we arrived on the doorstep at about 6.00 p.m. To our dismay we had somehow not managed to get our request to bring the dogs with us clear, and they were not expecting them! Winston exclaimed "They are as big as pit ponies! We can't have them in the house - they will have to stay in the car!" We were appalled. We thought of our

129

pampered puppies having a cold night in the car doing heaven knows what mischief in their frustration at being imprisoned. We chatted it over and reached a compromise. We would all go for a walk along the beach, with their three and our two, and, if they all got on, the decision might be reconsidered. (Apparently when Max arrived he had immediately told Brock that he was boss, so look out) Brock, who in his own mind is a lion, was having none of it and things got a bit stormy. Max treats ours just the same but they roll on their backs to indicate that he is boss and all is well. Brock wasted no time in telling Tom and Gill their fortune, in spite of the difference in size, but they are very easy going so accepted his authority without argument. They had a lovely romp together and returned the best of friends.

The Isle of Arran lies just across the sea and the sun was setting, lighting the clouds and lining them with gold. A brief break allowed a shaft of light to catch the waves as they rolled in, each one dispersing into a million sparkling droplets before breaking on the sand. When we said how wonderful it must be to have this magic outside their windows they suggested we watched the weather charts for South West Scotland before we got too envious! Rain and gales are the normal fare but evenings and sunsets like this one do make up for it.

When we got back Winston and Elizabeth relented and said they could come in, still on trial. We did not really blame them for their caution, as they have a beautiful house. We had told them as we walked on the sand how well the dogs had behaved on holiday, hardly put a paw wrong in fact, in spite of the plethora of knick-knacks just waiting to be knocked over in the colonial style bungalow in particular! Bedtime came and Elizabeth watched them hurtle upstairs with great misgivings, but all was well, we put their 'bed' rugs on the floor and they settled down like two black lambs. I slept lightly ready to spring into action should anyone be sick, newspaper at the ready, but it was not needed.

Next morning, Friday, I spent helping Elizabeth to plant the new plants. In the afternoon she and I planned to go to a flower festival, we went in our car and took all the dogs with us. Winston and David were off to enjoy a round of golf and left us to it. On the way we popped in to the retirement home where Mother is a resident, to say hello and knowing she wanted to see the boys after hearing about their exploits for over a year, they came too. Owing to their exuberance and size they had a mixed reception from the other residents, who, were sitting in the entrance hall. Mother was in her room and we surprised her. She was thrilled to see me and the dogs, they would make a splendid conversation piece for her for weeks! We stayed a while and then made arrangements to pick her up next day around 11.00 a.m. and take her back for lunch, then off we went.

The flower-decked church was lovely, Elizabeth and I had a good old natter to each other and caught up on the gossip without our men folk butting in, pretending to be bored. The afternoon flew by. We had another happy evening all together and a peaceful night. The dogs were being so angelic that we all relaxed, assuming that is how they would stay!

The rain beating on the skylight window woke us but by the time we had had some breakfast it had eased up and we volunteered to take all the dogs out while Winston and Elizabeth prepared the lunch. My brother likes cooking too, he was making steak and kidney pudding with leeks and tatties, a great favourite with everyone. By the time we got back he had gone to pick Mother up from her retirement home. We were all wet, so it was into the utility room for a major towelling and paw wiping session, twenty paws inspected and passed clean before we went into the house. Elizabeth is incredible, in spite of having five animals and a very wet climate she keeps the floors spotless, and the cream carpet in the hall and lounge always looks as if it is new. I am filled with admiration when I think of the state my home gets into, and I promise myself that I will try harder when I get back. For a while I do, but it wears off! We were just ready when Winston returned with Mother, whom he shepherded up the two steps and into the lounge to take her usual place on the sofa then he gave us all a drink. Mother had Cinzano in an elegant cut glass whisky tumbler and Elizabeth had her sherry in the kitchen, as there were urgent things to do! Then disaster struck for the first time, Mother misjudged the position of her glass and sent it flying. It smashed (ouch!) and there was glass and Cinzano all over the cream carpet, oh dear! In order to avoid upsetting Elizabeth, Winston tried to pick up the pieces and mop up, but Mother's distressed apologies reached her ears and she hurried in to see what had happened. She took in the scene and instantly cloths and bowls appeared and the carpet was rubbed back to its pristine condition. Elizabeth went back to her lunch preparations, her back view saying volumes! This visit was to test the carpet, and Elizabeth's patience to the limit. Winston followed her out hoping to pour oil on troubled waters but we could hear him getting a good ticking off for not watching Mother more closely, knowing that she has very bad sight. He stayed in the kitchen helping with the last stages of lunch and as the doors between us were open we suddenly heard an expletive from him not used except in dire stress. It transpired that he had tried to pick up a very hot dish of buttered leaks, burnt his hand and poured some leeks and lots of butter all over the floor, he managed to save the dish and most of the contents but great was the outcry at his carelessness. Elizabeth made it clear that he had made the mess, and he could jolly well clear it up! The meal was delicious and with full tummies and a good red wine to aid digestion the atmosphere soon relaxed.

After lunch we left Mother snoozing and Elizabeth and I plus the five dogs again went on a rose hunt. We were unsuccessful and to add to our frustration when we returned to the car the dogs had been having a party. The Jack Russells had found several bars of chocolate and some peppermints in the front door pocket which is safe from Tom and Gill as neither would have been able to get their big noses into the narrow opening - the terriers had no such difficulty. There was chocolate on the upholstery, bits of chewed paper and fluffy mints (that had been licked and discarded) were everywhere.

When we got back Winston gave us a glass of mulled wine which we were enjoying very much until David moved awkwardly and over went his glass. The cream carpet suffered again! Not surprisingly Elizabeth hit the roof this time, and offers of help and grovelling apologies did nothing to placate her. Small wonder she was upset at this further sabotage of her carpet. Like a whirlwind she scrubbed and rubbed it back to normal. Then David and I did a really stupid thing, we offered to run Mother back. We were trying to be helpful but we never considered how the dogs would feel being suddenly left behind. They did not know it was only for ten minutes or so. They were quite sure we had gone forever! In their excitement and relief in seeing us return they leaped madly about and knocked over the hall table, complete with flower arrangement, onto the cream carpet!

We looked at each other in horrified disbelief, whatever else could possibly happen? Elizabeth had not really calmed down from the wine episode and now this! We took the dogs and fled into the lounge, where we sat in silence listening to the sounds from the hall - suddenly there was another crash. Elizabeth herself had knocked over a bowl of pot-pourri that had been beside the phone. This time the vacuum cleaner was needed and the noise of it added another element of tension to the already electric atmosphere. My brother, aiming to help, made the sandwiches for supper, during which the conversation was confined to staccato remarks and monosyllabic answers. The dogs sensing the mood were very subdued now and rather than risk any further disasters we said our goodnights and went to bed although it was barely 10.00 p.m. Little did we know that there was worse to come!

Once upstairs I went into the bathroom first while David stayed in the bedroom with the boys; they were not ready for bed so soon and had not really had much exercise because the weather had been so foul. Whether the bout of horseplay that suddenly developed was because of this, or a release from the tension downstairs, we shall never know. When I came back to the bedroom they were really hyped up and wrestling energetically. They took no notice of orders to simmer down and, before I could save it, they cannoned into a cheval mirror, knocking it sideways into the wall beside the door. Miraculously it did not break but the corner of the frame knocked two holes in the wall the size of a 50p and 20p piece respectively. They were appallingly obvious just below the light switch. The wall was a partition and only made of plaster board, possibly if it had been really solid the mirror would have cracked too, who knows. The crash frightened and subdued the contestants, and when David came back from the bathroom I was waiting for either Winston or Elizabeth to come flying in to see what had happened now, but incredibly they had not heard and we were too cowardly to confront them until morning.

We did not sleep well. We were glad we were going home. We had a whispered argument about when to confess. With morning tea? Or at the very last moment before we left? And who should break the news? I got the short straw and decided to tell Winston in the kitchen before he brought us tea and saw for himself. He was understandably upset. There was no more emulsion paint left to disguise a repair and it would probably mean re-doing the whole room. They do a great deal of entertaining and the guest room was often in use. Oh dear, oh dear, I felt so sorry but what is done cannot be undone; he said I must own up to Elizabeth myself! I did, and took my verbal beating like a man, knowing I deserved it. If we had tails, they would have been between our legs! David and I are very fond of my sister in law and hated leaving like this; but I wrote to her the moment we got home to say how very sorry we both were, and I am glad to say we are still best of friends and have stayed with them many times since, but never again have we taken the dogs with us!

Chapter 15

WINTER INTERLUDE

It is early November now and the autumn leaves, which have coloured particularly well this year, are nearly all down, so we are having childish fun scuffing through great drifts of them. In the garden fallen leaves are treasure trove to be stored in sacks until they become black magic - leafmold. The stuff that will make a wooden spoon grow roots! Just lately our walks in the park have been singularly uneventful; the dogs too like rooting about in the leaves. Today was different as their arch enemy, the terrier behind the subterranean double glazing, had actually managed to move it slightly earlier this week when he got even more carried away than usual, and I was a bit afraid that he might tunnel out to attack us. We tried to sneak past, but he heard us and his barking alerted the small aggressive Spaniel a few doors up. His elderly mistress usually calls him in out of harm's way, but today she did not hear the rumpus. The boys always sharpen their step as we approach his domain, hoping to catch him and teach him to mind his manners. Today they had their chance, there he was, dancing up and down with rage behind his gates as he barked threats at them. With one accord they barged the gate. The Haltis were useless for once and I was hurled into the hedge as our combined weight pinged it open and in they charged, exchanging threat for threat. The little fellow bravely stood his ground but Gill bowled him over, then stood over him. That was too much, he became quivering rug of submission; meanwhile I was painfully unpicking myself from the hedge when the old lady opened the door and the little dog sped thankfully to safety indoors. I apologised and quickly removed us from the scene - no blood spilt.

Up at the airport next day you could lean on the wind. Making progress was slow. The flooded playing fields were once again the resting place for hundreds of gulls. What a challenge! The dogs took off in pursuit, and the poor tired birds flapped reluctantly into the air at the last possible minute, to land again further away, only to be chased into the air again. The wild flower areas have disappeared under water, while the hollows are so full that our wellies are in danger of drowning! The boys cared not that they were soaked to the skin and, having tired of seagull chasing turned to their favourite pastime - digging. They got so plastered that we were reluctant to let them into the car. We have given up trying to keep it clean or even dry!

The year is flying. The weather has improved at last. We have had three dry days in a row and it was a white sparkly world that greeted us this morning. We hunted for our furry hats with ear flaps before we ventured out. The car complained at being taken out of the garage, by steaming up as soon as we put the dogs in. We only got a few yards along the road when we were forced to stop again and wait for the engine to warm up. To add to the problem the low sun hit us straight in the eyes as we rounded the corner, totally blinding us. It was a glorious day, all the cars parked in the road were wearing ice jackets. Our steering was suspiciously light - caution was called for!

The grass was crunchy, each blade coated with ice crystals. The dogs made patterns as they circled round. There were no gulls today but the frosty air stimulated them to run faster and faster. Their panting breath hung in clouds behind them. We wrapped our scarves closely round our necks and enjoyed the clean crisp air. Not only was the scene beautiful to look at, it was also too hard to dig and we actually got home as clean as we were when we started!

Chapter 16

'CHRISTMAS'S COMING, THE GEESE ARE GETTING FAT'

Back home again the usual routine was soon re-established, but the problem of them not coming when called was getting bad again and we were at a loss once more to know how to tackle it. Tom is worse. He knows, when we are really cross, that he will be smacked, so he plays "grandmother's footsteps", plodding along about fifty feet in our rear, with hanging head, hanging tail and looking the picture of woe. If we stop, he stops and if we attempt to go back for him he runs off again. Gill is the opposite; he does come eventually and then, glowing with virtue, bounces along in front with "Oh what a good boy am I" written all over him. Doggy friends give conflicting advice; some say smack, others say coax and reward. We have tried both with little success, so now we just shout at them and hope for better things. "They are still babies", we tell ourselves.

Christmas is approaching; the days are short and dark and all walks, apart from the park, are very muddy. My kitchen floor is a nightmare to keep clean; brown mud shows as much on the yellow squares as it does on the black- I cannot win! Now, I just wash it everyday, remembering wistfully how nice it used to look, before they arrived on the scene; now it always looks dingy. What madness led us to take on these two hooligans? They cost a fortune, with food, vet bills, insurance, and hairdressing equipment. They make sure the house and garden are always a mess, either with their muddy persons or destructive garden games, not to mention their occasional "accidents" with unpredicted bodily functions!

We look at the room they take up and the happy knack they have of always being sound asleep in front of the cupboard you need to open urgently. We look at the way they worry us with their escapades!

We look at the time they take up with daily walks and monthly barbering sessions. On the other hand, they are very good house dogs and the daily walk is good for us, too. They make us laugh and we love them. We have to face it, they are our new family and we are hooked in spite of their numerous shortcomings.

We dare not pile our presents under the tree this year. We were very rash even to have a tree! We anchored it with guy ropes to heavy pieces of furniture but they have managed to barge it over twice, with the loss of several more precious glass ornaments, in spite of our efforts. The Christmas lights we left in the box. We kidded ourselves that by next year they would have steadied down and we could do all our traditional things - we are both great optimists!

The turkey, a fresh farm one, aroused great interest in dogs and cats alike. I was watched unwinkingly as I stuffed and prepared it for the oven. Linka and Tabs sat on the high stools, while the boys were on the floor with their leather snouts inches away from the action on the work top. I cut up the crop, divided it between them and just kept the liver and neck for the gravy. The succulent pieces vanished down four throats and the cats, knowing that was that for today, went off on important cat business. The dogs, ever hopeful, stayed put and watched me store the finished bird in the cooker. The only safe place for it. They then volunteered for guard duty. Timid Puska missed out this time, but when it is cooked she will get an extra piece or two; she misses out fairly often, but her figure gives no clue to her deprivation, as she is curvaceous, to put it politely!

With all the preparations up to date we went for a super walk on Sundon hills. The weather had been frosty for several days and it has been bliss to have the boys return still clean. The "warm water in a bucket outside the door" routine was getting tedious. They raced around, the nip in the air making them even more energetic than usual. They sailed over the five-barred gate like springboks and raced up the other side of the barbed wire fence for a while, before rejoining us by hurdling that. Every time they do it we visualise cut tummies or legs, but they judge it perfectly. After about an hour we had had enough; they were still playing tag and doing circuits of the switchback field, but we were ready to return home and relax by the fire.

Christmas day I was up by 6.00 a.m. to put the oven on. The vegetables were all prepared, and there was just the table to lay and the actual cooking to do, so we could take things easy until the troops began to arrive at about 12 noon. It was another gorgeous day and everyone was in high spirits. While David dispensed drinks, presents were examined and put back on the pile to be opened after the main event - Christmas Dinner! The turkey was sending mouth watering smells from the kitchen and before long we were all enjoying it. Robyn and John had brought Jason and Sasha, and Robert and Rachael had Max with them, so with David, Jo and Jim we were nine humans and eight animals; it was just as well it was a large turkey! The mountain of food that had taken so long to prepare was soon all gone. The end of the Queen's speech was the sign to begin opening presents. The carpet soon disappeared under a mass of wrapping paper and happy squeaks and exclamations of surprise and pleasure came from all sides, to the accompaniment of tearing paper. Jason loves tearing paper; he holds it between his huge paws and shreds it into smaller and smaller pieces until he has reduced it to fragments. The others copied him until they found their hide chews, then the paper lost its interest. The mess was quite spectacular. It takes a long time to pick up small pieces of paper. They were too big to vacuum, so one task force attacked the lounge while another blitzed the kitchen. In a very short time order replaced chaos, and a walk was ordered to wake everyone up and give the dogs a break. All too soon the day was over.

We saw the New Year in with our neighbours - we alternate who entertains each year and can drink as much as we fancy with no driving to worry about, an excellent arrangement ! We decided to leave the dogs at home, not surprisingly as Jean's cats really do not appreciate their presence! They were left to their own devices for four hours. The longest time yet. It was with some trepidation that we unlocked the front door ! We were almost knocked off our feet by the vigour of their welcome. They had missed us so much, that they had not touched the hide chews we had left for a treat; but now we were back they settled down to attack them with enthusiasm. Not feeling very chipper after an excellent evening, I awoke on New Years Day to find two "cow pat" look- alikes on the lower hall floor. What a start to the year !The reason for the upset tummies, was the disappearance of a half pound of frozen butter last night. We had accidentally left it within range to thaw for next day. I noticed that the kitchen floor had an unusual gloss to it in the area by the cooker, but I did not realise why!

We were going to Robert and Rachael's for midday feasting on New Year's Day and this time we took them with us. Rachael has many talents, she is a superb cook and an accomplished needle woman, her latest achievement being new lounge curtains complete with drapes and tie-backs. We were very impressed and had hardly finished examining and admiring them when Tom cocked his leg and peed up them! I nearly died. What possessed him, goodness knows; they were banished to the garden in disgrace and the curtain was sponged with cold water and mopped up. We felt terrible about it, and I could have murdered him; however Rachael hid her feelings and they all stayed outside while we enjoyed a fantastic meal. The table looked a picture when we started, with lovely linen and glass; the napkins matched the cloth and the flower arrangement toned with it. My son is a lucky fellow! Rachael's family were there too, and we all had a hilarious afternoon playing silly games, but that "I have eaten too much" feeling was attacking us and, when a walk was suggested, everyone including the dogs (especially the dogs) voted yes! There are extensive woods right behind their house, which means a walk can be as long or short as you fancy, the only slight problem, as far as our hooligans are concerned, is the occasional presence of horses or sheep in neighbouring fields. Robert, being only too well aware of their shortcomings, had checked when he took Max for his early run and all the fields were empty.

We strolled along, all eight of us, scuffing the leaves and savouring the chilly air. The three dogs, free of their leads, happily investigated all the scents and sounds in the undergrowth. Then I suddenly became aware that we were two dogs short. I alerted the others and we all stopped and listened. Faintly, on the wind, we heard the sound of barking; Robert, who knows the woods like the back of this hand, ran to check the nearest field, where, sure enough, two very black sheep were playing tag with the rest! In front of us was a scrabbled tunnel under the wire, the fence having been no problem to our experienced diggers! James and Robert were over the top in a flash and running across the field to the sheep, who were becoming more and more agitated as they tried in vain to get away.

On the far side of the field was a pond and the panic-stricken sheep were getting nearer and nearer, until one actually plunged in and was struggling about in the middle. The dogs were no match for the boys, who soon caught them and dragged them back to us. While James man-handled them over the fence, Robert went back to rescue the sheep from the icy water. He waded in regardless of his best trousers, and hauled the poor thing back to the side and out. He was wet to his waist, but before we could all go home he dripped to the farm house to confess. James went with him and they found the farmer relaxing after his dinner. He had his boots and coat on in an instant and went back with Robert and James to check on the other sheep. Robert apologised and explained that he had checked the field earlier, to which the farmer replied that he had only put them in that field just before lunch. He forgave us anyway; maybe the sight of the stinking, sodden mess that Robert was in helped! Once again the boys had let us down, so we returned with our tails between our legs - not the dogs of course, they were full of beans, it had been huge fun, and they would choose their walks to be like that everyday!

It was hard to knuckle down to normal work after over a week of overeating, drinking and late nights, so I did not notice immediately that Tabs was poorly. She had refused food all day and stayed in her basket. Gently stroking did not produce the usual purr, in fact normally she purrs if you speak to her. I was very worried and cross with myself for not noticing before. I tried to tempt her with chicken liver, usually a great treat, but she was not interested. It was too late to go to the vet there and then, but I knew it had to be the first priority in the morning. Cats have a way of not looking ill until they are very ill. Racking my brain for inspiration to think of something I could do to help her, as a last hope I thought of Katalax as she might be constipated. I squeezed it straight into her mouth thinking that a blockage caused by a hair ball might be the problem and a slight over dose would do no harm.

Next morning was Friday and I awoke to an ominous smell. Tom had evidently had a problem too and the answer was all over the lower hall. It was another rubber gloves, bucket and mop job - ugh. The good news was that Tabs was shouting for her breakfast from outside the front door. The Katalax had done the trick! I then found that that was what had done the trick for Tom too! - he had stolen the whole tube from where I left it on the window sill and only the metal remnants were left! Never mind, Tabs was better!

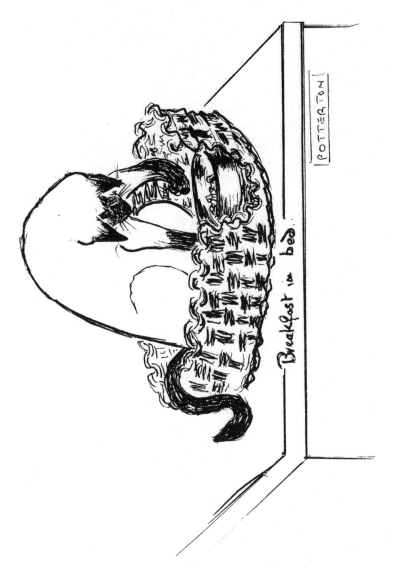

I feel a bit fragile.

143

Chapter 17

NEW KITCHENS PROVE INFECTIOUS

When Robyn and John came in, bursting with excitement to tell us that they had just chosen a super kitchen from the January sales at M.F.I., I was so impressed with their bargain buy that I twisted David's arm to come with me and look for us. There's no harm in looking is there? The kitchens displayed made ours look all of its twenty five years and we decided to take the plunge and have a new one ourselves. We made an appointment for the representative to come and see us and help us plan it. Now we had made the decision, the salesman had an easy job, and, after two hours of chatting, looking at his demonstration charts and measuring up, it was arranged that the actual fitters would do the work in early February. By the time he had gone, it was already mid-afternoon and the boys were getting restless, so I took them to the park, where they had a particularly energetic time squirreling, and were very reluctant to come home. I then had to pop out for some shopping. I did not have my usual quick look round for potential puppy hazards, which was a pity because on my return I found the remains of a box of brandy snaps I had not put away!

The next job was to feed all the animals. Tabatha was making the most of an indisposition and refused to eat with the others. She sat very straight and tall in the basket and indicated she wanted her food 'in bed'. Once I had put the bowl beside her, she graciously condescended to eat a little! The show of temperament was for my benefit; once I left the scene she tucked in and, on my return after our supper, it had all gone. I tucked her under my arm and brought her up for a cuddle, sinking into my corner of the sofa with a sigh of pleasure at the jobs all done for the day, but it was not long before Tom and Gill came over to enquire solicitously after her health, only to be answered by the ever ready lightening paw and one scratched nose; naughty jealous puss!

Three days later we left the boys in the kitchen after their walk and went to choose the tiles. We completely forgot the other half of the lunch time chicken that had been too warm to put in the fridge and was left sitting in a Pyrex casserole on the top of the bread bin, in theory out of range. When we came back it was to find all that remained was broken glass, a greasy floor and pieces of foam sticking to everything, For good measure they had also shredded an elderly cushion and its innards were everywhere, so it must have been a very good game! Our first thoughts were of them and the injury they might have done themselves - cut paws or mouths. There was no trace of blood, so we thanked our stars for small mercies and started to clear up the mess.

January 27th, David's birthday, not that that had anything to do with it! It was a lovely sunny day and the cats know that our bed is a sun trap in the mornings. Linka at some stage early on did her trick of jumping up at the door handle, pulling it down with her weight and unlatching the door. She is the only cat we have had who has been able to do this; her two daughters never try in spite of seeing her demonstrate the technique time after time. Anyway Madame must have led a posse on tip-toe up to our bedroom, past the sleeping dogs, and let them all in sometime before I left for work. They are cunning enough to hide under the bed until I have gone and the coast is clear, before emerging and taking over the bed. All morning they lay in a pile, bathed in sunshine on the duvet. They looked so sweet that it was hard to evict them, but I felt that after being shut in all morning it would be wise, so I hardened my heart and hoofed them out into the garden. Revenge is sweet; after lunch I put my wellies on prior to dog walking and someone had been sick from the penthouse straight into my boot. I did not discover it until I put it on! The dogs were really wicked on their walk, raiding the litter bins for discarded overnight takeaway. They ran off out of sight three times and totally ignored our calls as usual. Once we did get hold of them it was leads on and home, with a good ticking off. It has no effect but we feel we need to make a gesture!

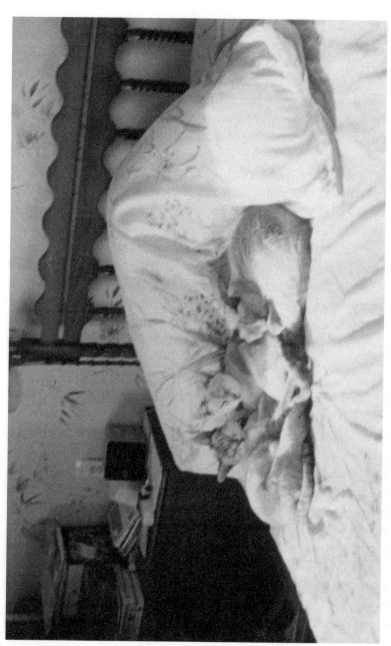

A pussy pile.

Chicken and chips?

At last the kitchen people were due to start. We were camping in the dining room, with the essentials i.e. the ketchup, tea/coffee gear and microwave on the trolley, everything else in boxes all around, it was very chaotic. They estimate that it will take a week to ten days; it was going to be a very long week, I suspected .The fitters, a husband and wife team, made friends with the dogs immediately and encouraged them into the kitchen to help! We, however, were banned from entering and had to hold any necessary conversation through the hatch!!! The job was finished in just over a week; oh the joy to have lots more cupboard space! My bin is now inside the door of the sink cupboard and really dog proof. The countless times I have found the contents of the old one all over the floor, in spite of all my efforts to fool them by wedging it under the work-top, only to see them push it out with their noses. I also tried wiring the swing lid on, no good, in fact I was stumped; this will be marvellous. Robyn gave me a lecture about not leaving garden gear all over my new tops. No paint brushes soaking in jam-jars, or balls of twine and secateurs, will be allowed. I did wonder whose kitchen it was, but she has a point, I will try to be tidy!

I re-housed all my equipment, gloating over the carousel cupboard and the pull-out shelf unit. I stored everything away while David tackled the decorating. As the walls are either covered in cupboard or tiles the area to be emulsioned was very small, just the ceiling and a bit above the windows and door. He had just started to gloss paint the radiator by the door when we had unexpected visitors. An old school friend who now lives in Australia was, unknown to me, staying for a few days with another friend of mine and they had come to say hello and see the garden. I shut the door on David and took them on the usual tour around. Then I simply had to offer them a cuppa, kitchen chaos or not. When I explained, they insisted on seeing the new domain. With great misgivings, thinking of the wet paint, I gingerly opened the door. David was just behind it - he would be! Gill, who had been trying to see what was going on all day, pushed past everyone, neatly wiping himself along the wet paint and transferring it to the next door cupboard. David looked volumes at me and I looked back, trying to indicate that I was a mere pawn in the hands of fate! The visitors seemed oblivious of the problems that they had just caused and enthused about the kitchen, while I searched frantically for the "better" mugs. I soon abandoned the search and we used kitchen ones and non-matching plates. All I really wanted to do was to catch Gill and clean him up before he spread himself further afield. He was nowhere to be seen - oh dear!

David did not join the impromptu tea party, as he was cleaning up paint and seething at the disastrous interruption. As soon as the guests had gone I hurried to soothe him and explain that I had had no choice, because once I had apologised to the visitors for the lack of hospitality and explained the reason, matters were taken out of my hands. The next task was to feed the animals; the cats got theirs first, downstairs as usual, and I was just tipping dog food into the first bowl when a crash from below sent me flying downstairs again to investigate. Dear, dear dogs; one of them had opened the utility room door, which in my state of mind I had neglected to bolt, and had then jumped at the draining board to reach the cat food, in doing so he had put his paw firmly on the sticky lid of the paint tin which was lying there. He was at that very moment decorating the new flooring and red stair-carpet with tasteful white paw prints as he fled from punishment. Stealing cat food is a major crime, and he was not waiting to see what I would do to him. Fortunately, the dining room balcony door was open and out he went. I was close on his heels and I shut it firmly before going in search of white spirit and cleaning rags! Once we had removed all the unwanted paint and repainted the radiator, we had a jolly good laugh about the whole episode. Tom and Gill carried their white decorations until their next clip. Thank God for a sense of humour!

Chapter 18

THE CASUALTY

March, and it is snowing hard. I shall put off the walk until after lunch, it can only improve. Wrong! The wind has got up and the snow is coming horizontally at us. I dressed for it in warm waterproofs and my wide brimmed waxed hat, but,with a dog in each hand, I have no hand left to hold my hat on! I put my head down and got on with it. The pavements were already white, it was slushy, but still coming down fast and furious. At least all the cats will be indoors! By the time we reached the park the dogs were white too, in spite of frequent shaking sessions. The wind was icy, my face stung and the wet was creeping down my neck. Right from the moment I let them go, they went mad, they rushed to and fro,they ate it, they dug in it, they even rolled in it!

I was ignored as usual. I just followed the path and left them to get on with it.When I rounded the corner into Bells Close, the wind was at a new angle and was driving the scything sleet straight at me. To add to my misery they both vanished. The ten minutes before they returned felt like an hour and I had had enough. I coaxed them with a biscuit, intending to put their leads on and go home; although we had only done half the walk enough was enough. I got Tom anchored and Gill was actually waiting his turn. I turned round to him and saw with concern that he was bleeding from a cut on his pad. It looked awful but I hoped it was the snow making it look worse than it was. I did not have even a hanky to bandage it so we headed home as fast as we could. He was bleeding so much he was splashing my shoes as well as leaving a scarlet trail in the snow. Once home before I did anything I had a good look a his foot. He had a deep gash across two pads, he must have stood on a bottle or something. It obviously needed urgent stitches!!

I ran to the phone and as I bent over to look up the surgery number, an avalanche of melting snow slipped off the brim of my hat all over the directory and phone! The nurse, on hearing my problem and I suspect detecting some panic in my voice, advised me, in a soothing tone, to hold a pad of cotton wool firmly on the wound until it stopped bleeding. It might take two or three minutes - she should see it!! She then suggested that I made myself a cup of tea. Oh, and if I was still worried bring him down in about an hour; the vets were all in theatre at the moment and not available. I grabbed cotton wool and crepe bandage and went back to him, to find the old rug lavishly decorated with blood already - I bound his paw as tightly as I dare, and he kept still and let me! I think he must have been in some pain by then. I stopped applying the pressure for just long enough to strip off my sodden coat and trousers and put my old gardening ones on - they were hanging there handy in the utility room which was the scene of the operation. In that minute the blood had come through the bandage. I gave them a brief towelling. They too were wringing wet in spite of some vigorous shaking, then I put the towels on the floor to mop up the blood and snow; there was blood everywhere. Tom did his best to clean his brother up, assiduously licking him, but it was a hopeless task. I got the car out, then went back and put the foot in a plastic bag, with a rubber band tightly round his wrist. I was sure once they saw how much blood he was losing they would do something rather more quickly than an hour! As I hoped, the blood filled plastic bag produced instant action. A lady vet we did not know asked how recently he had eaten (not since yesterday) and took him off to be stitched.

The afternoon passed slowly, Tom never left my side; he was really upset and it was sweet to see how much he missed his brother. At five we phoned as instructed , but he was too muzzy to come home yet - we must be patient for another hour. Before then David came home from work and listened to the tale of woe.Then we went together to fetch him.He came to greet us, tail wagging, pleased to be going home. He was limping badly and bandaged to his elbow. The snow had turned to rain and without the poly- bag we got the dressing a bit wet straight away. The odd thing was that when Tom ran to greet him, Gill growled and curled his lip, a thing he had never done before. We were forced to separate them. Tom did not understand and hated being kept away, but Gill soon fell asleep in front of the fire and we let Tom in again. He lay beside, but not quite touching him, with his eyes never leaving him, for ages, until he too fell asleep. We decided to let them sleep on the bedroom floor in the hope that I would hear if he started to take his dressing off in the night. Ever since the children were babies I have been able to programme myself to wake if necessary; I believe lots of mums can do it, it can be very useful! Lots of fathers, on the other hand, have the knack of sleeping through everything!

I woke at four to hear him chewing himself. I jumped out of bed, shouting at him as I hurried to put on the light. He had already removed about four inches of sticking plaster. I got the scissors and cut off the frilly edge and added more plaster. By the time I had sorted him out. I was wide awake and cold, so I cuddled up to my nice warm husband, who had not budged in spite of the noise and lights! He could do his bit by warming me up!

Sleep would not come and I lay trying to remember how we coped last time we had a similar problem. We still had one usable "lampshade" somewhere, the other got chewed up, I recall; the bitter tasting spray was still in the cupboard. I also remembered putting an extra layer of tubular bandage over the whole paw as a front line of defence and to keep it clean. With these options churning round in my head I dozed off and woke to hear Sarah Kennedy talking about her new book about terrible pets. I reflected that our pair's escapades would need a book on their own!

The next day I kept them separated and put the lampshade collar on Gill before I went to work. All was well at lunch time, and I took Tom out on his own for a short walk before I got started on some

Oh dear - Tom helps Gill get his bandage off - so he has a lampshade too!

urgent garden jobs. My seedlings urgently needed pricking out. Half an hour later I emerged from the greenhouse to find the lawn strewn with bits of dressing and Gill working on the final piece, which meant he had exposed all the stitches; just a band round his ankle was all that remained! I hauled him indoors, trying to keep his foot off the ground as we went. As I began to assemble strapping, scissors, sterile dressing, etc. I was most relieved to see David arrive home. I called for help and between us we made a good job of it. It was a bit like trying to sellotape a live parcel! To his disgust we then put the lampshade back; he resisted with all his might, and when we finally got it fixed he entertained us with his efforts to rid himself of the horrid thing. He walked backwards, weaving about as he tried to leave it behind, he twisted and shook, but all in vain. When he had convinced himself that it was there to stay, he flopped down miserably on the kitchen floor and watched me reproachfully as I prepared our meal.

Later, when I collapsed on the sofa, he followed me and most of him sat on my lap - the rest overflowed onto the cushions. Although we do not allow them on the furniture, he knew instinctively that today he was in with a good chance! I cuddled him for two hours, by which time I was squashed flat and so stiff I could not move anyway! Tabatha was not to be cheated of her usual position and claimed the few inches of me that protruded from under the black blanket, settling just below my chin, after much turning and twisting to show her displeasure at having to play second fiddle!

It is three days now since the accident and he has had the bandages off twice. I have invented a new dressing - after strapping it in the conventional way I have been covering it with shiny plastic parcel tape - it is very hard to find an end to pull and it is waterproof !If it stayed on very long he would get soggy underneath it, but there is not much chance of that! It is beginning to heal,so he is not limping and he is enjoying a game with Tom. Day five, he had it off again and it is looking much better, although it is still bleeding a

'You can larah'

What are you doing in there?

155

little. After a very trying morning at work I reinforced my sentiments about preferring animals to people - even tear-aways like our two! But that was before I got home. In a weak moment I had let Tabatha stay on my bed, to make up for all the fuss HE was getting. What had Gill done? He had caught the edge of my full length mirror with the front edge of his protective plastic cone and there it lay, in a thousand pieces, sparkling prettily in the shag pile . Have you ever tried to get little bits of anything out of elderly shag pile? First I hand picked the bigger bits, then I used the nozzle on the vacuum to get the rest. Three times I went over it and still little pieces twinkled at me, only to vanish when I tried to pick them up. How am I going to remember to put my slippers on before crossing the danger zone in the middle of the night to visit the loo!

Lunch was very late. David has twisted his knee, as if we haven't enough problems! At any rate it is Saturday, so he can sit and rest it - and baby sit Gill at the same time while I take Tom out. I went back to the spot where Gill did the damage, to see if I could find the guilty bottle or whatever it was. I found it, what a sight! Someone, presumably a workman, had been creating a bank and had unearthed a dump of broken window glass, which was sticking up out of the soil. No wonder it was such a wicked cut. Tom was over the far side of the park, chasing squirrels and not likely to come near me for some time, so I picked up some of the bigger pieces and binned them, but it was a futile exercise as the ground was peppered with shards, too much for me to make much impression on it. When we were home again, I sat down and wrote a strong letter to the parks department, requesting an instant clean up before another dog or child came to grief, and drove down to deliver it for priority attention on Monday morning.They had done the job by next day, thank goodness.

April fools' day, not an omen I hope, as Jo and I are expecting a lady who makes really lovely wedding bouquets. I had a quick clear up in the lounge, removing some tired daffodils, a shoe, a kitchen towel, a lonely sock and sundry other doggy additions to the décor.

Non-doggy people just don't understand! She was punctual and, much to their disgust, I shut them out. They immediately appeared at the window, noses pressed to the glass, trying to hypnotise us to let them in. She then spoilt all my disciplinary efforts by going to the window and exclaiming "Oh aren't they lovely - I love dogs!" Whereupon Jo let them in and they took over. Gill in particular made a huge fuss of her; he sat beside her leaning heavily against her knees and gazed into her eyes. She melted under his charm and hugged and cuddled him. I was not heartless enough to question that the chocolate biscuit she had on her plate had anything to do with this show of affection! We decided after much discussion how the all important bouquet was to look, and she made her departure. Jo and I made a day of it; we booked the Rolls and went again to look at the lovely old church where it should all be happening in September. We left the dogs at home, which was a mistake. Gill had his dressing off for the fifth time. I am at a loss to think of more ways to defeat his efforts. He is managing to push his bonnet down his giraffe - like neck to get his nose out far enough to reach his paw. It was three-forty a.m. when David dug me in the ribs and said "He's getting it off again!" I hauled myself back to life, found the gear and redid it for the sixth time. He is beginning to enjoy this exclusive treatment. He sits as good as gold while I wrap him up. If only I could get through to him that it is not a game to see how long it takes him to get off again! It is very seldom that I can use the crepe bandage twice, as it is so badly chewed. So far we have caught him before he has attacked the stitches but that is going to be the next problem; it is not a week, until tomorrow, since he did it, so we could be back to square one if he succeeds.

The snow is quite forgotten, the weather has done a U-turn and the garden is visibly growing under the warm sunshine; everything needs doing at once. The ivy has shot up the house wall and is taking over the guttering, which will need a ladder to reach, the lawn is due for its feed and weed treatment and there are weeds everywhere; what shall I do first? Indoors it is spring cleaning time, what a hope! I did make a gesture by taking down the lounge curtains, removing the hooks and putting them one at a time into the machine. Halfway through the third wash the machine went on strike. That was all I needed. I hauled out the sodden dead weight, dumped it in the bath for a last rinse and then, leaving a wet trail behind me, I flopped it over the rotary drier to drip. My S.O.S. to the engineer was answered on Tuesday and, while I got to grips with the last curtain, David had his first solo attempt at repackaging Gill. The result looked like something out of a Monty Python film but to David's delight it stayed on all day!

We were due to return to the surgery on Thursday; the appointment was 9.15 a.m. and we were there early, resplendent in our bonnet and parcel tape. Poor Gill was subject to some amusement from the nurses, thanks to our unorthodox first aid. We chatted to other patients while we waited. The elderly Siamese had bad constipation. The very old Whippet needed his nails cut. The cheeky young black tom was soon to be much less cheeky - a good thing that he does not know he is about to be fixed!

Then it was our turn. The deft way that Owen dealt with a wriggling paw and miles of sticking plaster was a joy to see. The stitches are not ready to come out yet; we are to return next week. We have a new lampshade a size bigger. Once in the car Gill did his best to dodge away from me, but I cornered him and shoved it over his ears. Poor lad, it is huge and he is quite unable to steer through a door or go downstairs without pranging it, which at the rate he is usually travelling must give him quite a headache. Just before bedtime he managed to knock over a large plant stand that was loaded with plants. There was earth, plants and broken pots everywhere. I was not impressed! This new collar is more of a problem than it is worth. He is still managing to get at his foot but he can't get through anything smaller than the garage door without a collision. The wallpaper down the stairs is in a terrible state where he keeps scraping it. I took it off and explained to him, man to man, why he has had to wear it and that if he can manage to leave his paw alone I will not put it back. I obviously did not expect this to work, but incredibly he has had it off less frequently since our chat! As far as I am concerned it is a relief not to have the trail of destruction that he was leaving in his wake as he bulldozed every thing more than three feet off the ground; we are both feeling much better! The dressing sessions are now the highlights of Gill's day. I just say - "oh dear we had better go and do your paw again" - and he trots happily ahead of me into the kitchen. I follow, shutting the door on Tom, who then goes into the dining room and puts his paws on the serving hatch, so that he can be sure that treats of an edible nature are not being administered behind his back! It is obvious that it will be ages before walks are on Gill's agenda unless I can make some kind of boot. I got some vinyl material and experimented. The first attempt was useless, it just fell off. I unpicked it, cut it down and tried again. I used Evostick and fin-ished with a shoe lace threaded round the ankle. It looked quite smart!

It is time to see Owen again, several of the stitches having been removed by the patient, who made it bleed again in the process, but the boot is doing a good job for the moment. I am expecting David to meet me in the waiting room; he should be able to get away by then. I shut Tom in the kitchen, to his dismay, and took Gill down to the surgery in his new boot. David was there before us and Gill was thrilled to see him !He put his paws on his shoulders and licked his nose; as David was standing up at the time, this was quite impressive!

We sat in a row. On my left, in the corner, was an inoffensive little man with a very small box on his knee - a mouse?- a budgie? David was on the other side of me, and around the full waiting room an assortment of dogs sat or stood by their owners, all studying each other with interest (dogs and owners that is).Gill gave the nearest dog - a black Labrador - a small growl just to make sure he knew who was in charge, then he stood in front of me, put his huge paws on my knees and huffed amiably into my face. After a minute or so, he leaned over towards the stranger with the mysterious box and stuck his nose in the poor man's ear. At this point I should have restrained him, but I knew his attentions were friendly and the little man's reactions were so comical that a devil in me let him carry on. He recoiled and leaned as far away as possible, but Gill's nose followed him and he was subjected to a slow, thorough sniffing session - ear to forehead, along his hair line and back to his ear for another checkup. He never once actually touched his victim. I was very naughty not to have stopped him, but it was so funny and, as the whole waiting room was watching the pantomine, I am ashamed to say I let him continue with his inspection. As Gill loomed over him, the man seemed to shrink. He must have been thankful at that point to hear his name called. As he ducked away, clutching his box, the whole room collapsed in laughter - they had been enjoying the poor man's discomfort and anxiety as much we had!

When our turn came, Owen approved the boot but shook his head over our account of the battle we have had to keep the wound covered. He said that only Dobermen rivalled Poodles for being bad patients. He removed the remaining stitches and said that he had better see him again in another two weeks. His boot worked like magic for two whole days, then he suddenly attacked it and it was goodbye boot. What now? There was just one tiny open place on each pad, and I tried sticking a circle of plaster directly on them. It seemed to work as he has not tried to get them off, in fact he does not seem aware that they are there. I have to renew them very frequently but each time it looks a little better, so perhaps we are winning at last!

It is three weeks now since it happened and Easter is here. We went to morning service at the church where Joanne's wedding is planned to take place in September. It is very old and atmospheric, it will be a lovely setting.

Easter Monday I went downstairs early in bare feet, without putting the light on, and stood in a squishy poo - UGH! I hopped to the bathroom, put my foot in the loo and flushed, then I finished it off with toilet paper. Next I had to face the remaining mess on the floor. When it was done I called them; they trotted to me and I pointed to the mess and said in a fierce voice WHO DID THAT? Tom fled and Gill stayed, looking virtuous, so I knew the answer!

Gill's foot is better at last but he now has a skin infection under his chin which requires anointing with cream several times a day; I wonder what he will think up next!

Chapter 19

THE GARDEN IN THE NEWS

I had an exciting time the other day when I was asked by a friend to stand in for him on a local radio phone in programme about gardening. It went splendidly. I was not thrown by a couple of catch questions and came home on a high. I was offered the spot permanently, but as no payment was attached (just glory) I declined. My morning job, the garden and the dogs, take me all my time. It would take a substantial carrot to tempt me to take it on. This was not the only excitement of the week. I had a message to say that a B.B.C. researcher would like to see the garden tomorrow. She came and spent a long time, with me beside her answering questions, and then went round on her own. After which she said that she liked what she had seen, and if when they feature gardens in this area she would certainly be in touch; What a thrill! It is seven years now since we were on Gardeners' World.

It is August 11, Friday, Jo's wedding is only three weeks away - I am beginning to panic! Rachael's mother, Ann, phoned to say she has finished the cake, and we had just arranged to go over this afternoon to see it when the phone rang. It was Geoffrey Hamilton's son; he wanted to come to come and take pictures of the garden for Geoffrey's weekly feature in the Saturday Express supplement! And he wanted to come now!! I was thrilled and quickly organised a walk for the boys. The cake viewing was harder to fit in before 3.30 pm but our important visitor assured me that he was quite happy to be left to get on with it - in fact I got the feeling that he preferred it! He arrived in a Land Rover clad just in shorts and sandals; with the temperature in the 80's again it was very sensible. He had a good look round and expressed satisfaction with what he saw, but was unhappy about the harsh sun light. He said he would wait until the light was softer and at a lower angle. I made sure he had everything he needed and then we drove over to see the

Back of the house.

cake. It was beautiful! I knew it would be and had been looking forward to this moment; Ann had created a master piece. The three tiers were decorated with the most delicate sugar roses and carnations in the same cream and buff shades as the bouquet; loops of narrow ribbon in cream ochre and rust, cascaded from one layer to the next, linking them all together - it was exquisite.

We arrived home about 6pm to find our friend very busy with tripod etc. He had found lots to do and was still taking pictures well into the evening, using the setting sun to back light his shots. I cannot wait to see the result. It is to be in the Bank Holiday weekend edition. I was not disappointed; there was a full page of lovely photos and a super article by Geoffrey who had been to the garden to film "Gardener's World" in 1986. I treasure the memory of a charming and sincere man, totally in love with his plants and the wild life he encouraged into his garden with his environmentally friendly methods of gardening .

The big day is here and it is raining! Rain before 7am fine before 11am, the old saying proved right again. We had minor panics - the button-holes arrived late, the hairdressing took too long thanks to Jo's long locks, but the bride and her maids were ready at last. The dress was reminiscent of "Les Sylphides." It was in cream with a fitted bodice and a very full gauzy skirt. Joanne wore her auburn hair in a long plait twined with pearls . More pearls kept her veil in place in a single band across her forehead. She looked heart - stoppingly beautiful. Most mothers looking at their daughters on their wedding day get sentimental and I was no exception. Everything went smoothly after the early hiccups. The little church was decked with flowers, the service was moving and sincere; all the guests singing with enthusiam made a wonderful atmosphere and I found myself wiping away a tear.

Some of the guests were staying overnight and I had been cleaning and baking in preparation. There was one nasty moment when I was washing the white wallpaper at the top of the stairs (it was

We can have a bit of a sit down now.

rather muddy, I cannot think why) when Tom heard the cat flap bang and he and Gill zoomed downstairs in their usual headlong fashion, catching my bucket of soapy water on the way past and sending it in a mad pirouette towards the carpet. I was just too far away to catch it and I watched in horror, but this time all was well and it stayed upright on the brink - whew!

The dogs were a big hit with the visitors and got spoiled rotten. They were in kennels yesterday as we dare not risk their robust carryings on with all the finery and flowers to sabotage, so we turned a blind eye to the titbits that they scrounged shamelessly from everyone. Always seeking attention, Gill managed to sit on a wasp's nest in the garden; he rose rather quickly but did not seem to have been stung. Their coats are so thick his must have protected him!

Have they all gone?

Chapter 20

WE'RE ALL GOING TO THE ZOO TOMORROW
- ZOO TOMORROW - ZOO TOMORROW

We have the choice of two walks on Dunstable Downs. We can park on the top and track up and down the precipitous hills in a northerly direction or we can drive to the other end near the zoo and leave the car in the Bison Hill car park, which is above and overlooking the zoo. The first car parks were choc-a-bloc, after all it was August bank holiday and fine weather! All the world was there, walking dogs, flying kites and watching the gliders. We drove to Bison Hill, parked easily and had a splendid walk, meeting only a few walkers once we were away from the popular areas; the boys roamed a little and dug a little, and sniffed a lot, travelling at great speed through the long grass, with noses never rising from the ground. It was just their stumpy periscope like tails that allowed us to keep an eye on them. They were tired after an hour or so and we headed back to the car, as we too were tired. It was a lovely hot day. We wished we had brought something to drink. There were ice-cream vendors and a café down the other end, but Bison Hill did not qualify for such luxuries. The dogs trotted along with us for once and we did not bother to put leads on. How many times have I written that? As usual we lived to regret it.

As I mentioned, the car park branches off from the steep downward hill and goes equally steeply upwards to a plateau, from the edge of which both zoo and the snaking road are visible. Tom jumped straight into the car but Gill, his nose full of strange exciting zoo smells, stood gazing down. The next moment he is tearing down the track to the busy road, over it, up to the wire perimeter fence, where a wallaby was hopping happily along on the inside, minding its own business. It hopped a bit faster when it saw Gill, in fact it positively trampolined down the hill, staying near the fence. Gill followed as close as he could, barking his excitement and making mad dashes into the traffic, with resultant squealing brakes and bad language from the startled drivers. We slammed the car shut on poor innocent Tom and ran in pursuit - David went down the hill after the villain and I stood with one foot on the verge and one on the road, flapping my arms in a frantic attempt to warn the oncoming cars that there was a problem on the road ahead.

Meanwhile the stupid wallaby continued down the hill, near enough to the fence to keep Gill on the boil, and the merry chase continued, wallaby, Gill and, puffing and over-heating in the rear, David. The dear dog did not give up until he reached the T-junction half a mile (we clocked it later) away; even then he tried to avoid capture and David was forced to play tag before he gave himself up at last. The half mile down the hill after a good walk was knackering enough for a person of pensionable age not taken to running, the return, steeply up, reduced him to an exhausted, steaming wreck. Gill, who usually pulls when on a lead, was too tired to help. We had intended to call in on Robyn after our walk but I was too traumatised, after expecting every moment to hear brakes squeal and have an injured or killed dog and/or David on my hands, to even think straight. Totally shattered we went straight home!

September has arrived, the weather is still fine but the grass is heavy with dew and the sun is losing its power. The mushrooms continue to abound and we feast on them several times a week. Robyn and John are off to a steam rally this weekend and we shall be in charge of Jason and Sasha from Friday lunch-time. We went up to the airport on Saturday morning with all four; it was very quiet, a slight drizzle was falling and the more delicate dog walkers had elected to stay at home. They had a good romp and our two were marginally more obedient, thanks to the example set for them by Jason and Sasha.

After lunch we planned to leave them all in the garden and go on a manure gathering expedition to Totternhoe. We loaded the car with sacks, shovels and forks, bolted the side gates, just in case anyone called round, and let the dogs out before they realised that they were loose in the garden. As the weather was still a bit wet, we left the garage side door open for them to take shelter, if need be. We then went back through the house, locking behind us, and out of the front door. Just as we were getting into the car David remembered his gardening gloves were in the garage and he opened the main door without thinking - whoosh-whoosh! They were gone! Their first call was to Jean's to look for cat food. They then executed a merry zigzag down the road until at the bottom they found an open front door. Whoopee - in they rushed (not Jason or Sasha, they had nothing to do with this bad behaviour) but the lady who lives there has two German Shepherds and recognised them, so was not alarmed, just amazed! They gulped down stolen dog food - the owners luckily for them were shut in their garden, did a quick tour around the downstairs and rushed out. David paused to apologise and set off in pursuit again. I called and tempted them with chocolate biscuits and, as usual, greed won and I had them. After laborious unlocking and re-locking of gates, they were once again secure in the garden and we set off. By this time it was nearly four o'clock and the traffic was bad, but when we reached the field the ground was hard and dry and so was the manure, so we drove the car to the pile and lost no time in filling our plastic sacks. We managed to cram nineteen into the car in no time and were soon on our way home. We plan to go over again before the rain makes it heavy and hard work to gather.

Jean and Sean are away, so I fed their three cats. They played hard to get, and at last we put the food down and left them to it. We figured that if one missed out on this meal it would make sure it was on parade next time! Robert and Rachael are off on holiday too and next week the pen will be up again and we shall have eight cats and four dogs to look after!

Tuesday, the boiler man came to do a service and did not latch the gate properly, so my hooligans escaped again. The first I knew of it was when my other neighbour phoned, and not in the sweetest of tones said: "Your dogs are in my garden!" Oh dear, he is not always friendly anyway, because he insists that it is my cats that poo on his front lawn. I do not think it is, but I apologised profusely. This time I got a lecture on bringing up dogs - if only he knew! Meanwhile, the cat posse had been checking the kitchen. Having satisfied themselves that all was well, they returned to the warmth of the boiler and settled down for some serious sleeping. They probably thought that with all these lodgers in the garage, they might miss out on something if a sharp eye was not kept, so they had better have a good rest to be prepared for whatever hazards were on the way!

Chapter 21

TAT FOR TIT - THE BITER BIT

Yesterday I had a big family lunch to do. Winston and Elizabeth, plus Robert and Max, Robyn and John were all due to arrive around 12.30.p.m. Max and Robert were first and Max gave the boys "the treatment", which as usual reduced Tom to a jelly and caused Gill to wet himself with anxiety. That all over, the Scottish party arrived, complete with the three Jack Russell terriers, who quickly ran in and out and all over everywhere, barking their enthusiasm at being freed from the car after a long ride.

At 1.30p.m. I put the roast beef on the table, with the Yorkshire and loads of vegetables, and called everyone to come and take their place. There was a sudden cry from Robert "Oh No!" He had put his foot in a pile of "You know what" on the carpet. There were in fact three piles! Elizabeth was mortified. Hasty clearing up operations took place; the lunch was getting cold but the smell from under the table was terrible and had to be dealt with quickly!

The beef was a poem (I must remember to tell the butcher) with roast spuds, marrow, and squash, stir fried carrots and the very last runner beans completing the first course. Then Cornish clotted cream with fruit salad was welcomed, and demolished. Everybody said 'yum yum'. Elizabeth could not get over her dogs' misdemeanour. I found this highly amusing after the shambolic visit to them last year. We are all square now!

September is drawing to a close and tomorrow it is back to work for us. The boys knew as soon as we got dressed in normal clothes, as opposed to leisure wear, that it was no good badgering us for a walk, and they settled in the hall to sleep the morning away, dreaming doggy dreams until we returned at lunch time. They are so fit it is hard to tire them at all; down at the park they did circuit after circuit just for the sheer joy of it and still had to be checked constantly for pulling on the way home.

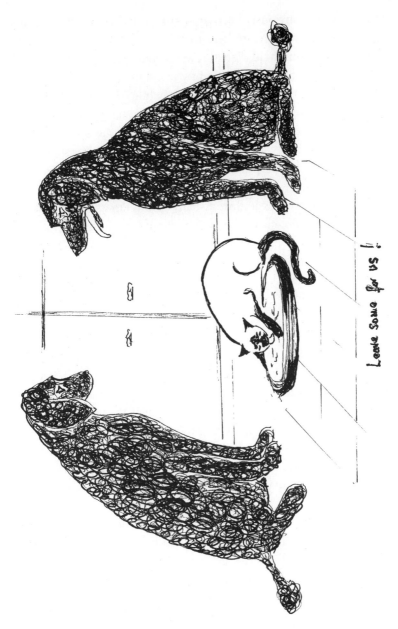

Tabatha exerts her rights.

The cats have obviously been discussing the dogs and have come to the decision that they are here to stay and cannot be allowed to dominate their household. Tabatha was voted leader of the trio and she demonstrated her new position by claiming the meat dish (as of old) and licking it on the kitchen floor while 'they' watched; they were allowed to see if there was any left when she had had enough. We were most amused. Linka is not far behind but she is still inclined to dive for cover if they get a bit too familiar, whereas Tabs stands her ground and hands out punishment if necessary. Poor Puska only watches from afar.

Unless the weather is foul we usually give them a longer walk on Saturdays and, although we knew they would get filthy after all the rain, we planned to bath them on our return anyway, so Maulden woods was our chosen destination. We had not been there for ages and it was the very last decent afternoon as the clocks go back tonight. They seemed to know they were in for a treat and were very excited in the car; the cunning blighters really do seem to recognise our regular routes, even if we go relatively infrequently. They had a wonderful time, chasing in and out of the trees, finding all the boggy spots but keeping fairly near to us until the last two hundred yards then, coinciding with the passing ranger, they thundered off deep into the woods. He stopped and hauled us over the coals for having uncontrolled dogs loose, frightening the wild life. He hung about for ages waiting for us to capture them, but what a hope! How they let us down! About a quarter of an hour later they crashed back, filthy, grinning and unrepentant; fortunately he had given up waiting and driven off. I felt inclined to point out that "one" the wild life has the woods to themselves ninety five percent of the time and "two" rabbits, hares, and muntjac all move much faster than they do and it must be good for them to get some exercise; the muntjac in particular are not very environmentally friendly anyway!

Today we are going to visit the friends who said "Oh you have got Standard Poodles, they have a great sense of humour" and then flatly refused to enlarge on the statement, which left us slightly apprehensive! We now know exactly what they meant!

We had to drive to Mansfield in Nottinghamshire, so we were up at the crack of dawn and out to the park with them. The autumn colours were still wonderful, the dampness adding to their intensity. We were quickly round, and back, which gave us time to groom them well for this special trip. They looked marginally better for it and they certainly enjoyed it. We arrived in good time and they were admired and fussed over, before being allowed to run in the dog proofed garden. We were amazed; they actually behaved perfectly, not a paw was put out of place. John our host sat for ages, with Gill leaning on his knee and gazing soulfully at him whilst having his tummy scratched! We dined greedily on Sue's delicious lunch, and later on her tea, and left reluctantly around 8.00p.m, feeling very full after a lovely gossipy happy day. Our euphoria was short lived; we had two very long hold ups on the M1 and when we finally reached home the cats were all on the drive, waiting very impatiently for their tea. We got a severe talking to before they sent us to Coventry! Back home at last, everything was inspected and someone cocked a leg over their own bed rugs and my wellies, but after the walk their tanks were nearly empty and it was only a token, thank goodness!

Not so next day when David let them into the bedroom to say good morning to me; Tom produced a lake over the corner of the bed, soaking the duvet, carpet and his pyjamas which were on the floor - yuck, but it does wake you up! It was only when I had dealt with this mess that David said "Oh by the way, Gill was sick in the lounge last night after you had gone to bed". And then added proudly "but don't worry, I cleaned it up!" - "What did you use?" I asked, fearing the worst. "The pie slice, hot water and Fairy Liquid," he said. Needless to say there was a large yellow stain which I set about with Vanish, but it did not vanish entirely. I hope the sun will finish the job for me; if only he had used cold water.

I still had to sort out the bedroom. I had mopped the carpet but the washing had still to be done. The cover and pyjamas went straight into the machine but the soiled corner of the duvet was a hands on job in the sink. I got it clean but managed to soak the floor and me in the process. It is king size and so heavy and unwieldy. I called David to help me hang it over the rack to drip. I was very late for work.

Chapter 22

DIRTY NAILS AND DUNGAREES

The walnut tree is loaded with nuts, even the squirrels cannot eat them all, although they are trying very hard! Tom sits for hours underneath, craning upwards to watch a blatant show off who is leaping happily from branch to branch, very visible but unreachable. To add insult to injury he drops bits of shell on Tom's head as he crunches and cracks his way through the harvest. I have picked up two buckets full of nuts from the ground, which will stain my fingers as I too chomp through them, but who cares! They are delicious!

The garden needs me badly after two weeks' neglect, but a good session of cutting down dead things and weeding will soon bring it to heel. To look on the bright side, there are still flowers to enjoy, Michealmas daisies in six different shades of blue and mauve, japanese anemones in pink and white, hardy fuchias everywhere, dripping with blooms and, the star of them all, a bed of nerine lilies, if the weather allows, which will stay looking fabulous until well into November. My creeper too, is flaming crimson; dew laden spider's webs, autumn's autograph, sparkle in the pale sun shine and the first fallen leaves stud the grass with yellow and red.

A task awaits us that we are not looking forward to; the compost heap needs rethinking. You are supposed to make your heap directly onto the soil (the book says) to allow worms and woodlice to get into it to aid its breakdown. The sides are made of breeze blocks, put together very messily by us a long time ago; we are no good at cementing but we managed to build a large double bunker that is still firm as a rock. The problem is that the earth underneath the compost is black and gorgeous and I cannot resist digging a bit more of it out each time and now it is more of a compost pit than a heap! We decided, book or no book, to make a solid concrete base with drainage holes. It is to this task that we are turning our energy as soon the garden is sorted out for the winter. The mature compost has been spread on the borders, leaving the stage clear for our DIY efforts. What satisfaction there is in seeing the lovely dark mulch protecting and feeding the soil, but what a rotten back-aching job it is to do! Frosts are now a nightly feature but we decided to go ahead, being careful to cover the wet concrete at night with some old carpet. When the job is done we can hibernate with clear consciences as far as the garden is concerned.

Yesterday the sun shone and the park was resplendent in its autumn colours. The dogs collected so much goose grass seed on their coats, and particularly on their noses, which looked like those licorice allsorts covered in 100's and1000's - all ready to spread in the garden! Hips and haws abound, we shall see if the prophesied hard winter will follow. Today it is a different world, the sky is uniform grey and a chilly wind is making us put up our collars and plunge our hands in our pockets. The colours of yesterday are hardly noticeable in the misty gloom. There is a hint of bonfire smoke in the air and winter feels very near; we shall be glad to be home in our nice warm house.

Rain and more rain. The dogs dug another hole in the lawn yesterday - David was furious! They just kept a safe distance from him until he had calmed down. My border got the same treatment but the carpet of clematis netting that I pegged down in the spring hampered them and it could have been worse. October half gone and still it rains. Two inches last night and more thunder - what is happening to the weather? I should have kept quiet; after two fine days the temperature plummeted to minus five overnight, reducing the busy-lizzies to slime, and finishing off the nerines for another year, and putting a substantial layer of ice on the pond. But the ground is too hard for the villains to dig, so every cloud has its silver lining!

Christmas is approaching with its problems over what to give to whom, and then shopping endlessly in crowded stores for the desired items. Next the feverish stocking up on food, finishing with enough to withstand a siege for a week, in spite of being invited out for two of the major meals. Like it or not it is all now upon us. It could easily be a white Christmas; already there has been a dusting of snow and in Scotland and in the northern islands several feet have fallen, bringing down power lines and trapping people in their cars. Several have died of hypothermia. To add to the general misery, temperatures are down to a record breaking minus 22%F. and the snow is so deep that power is unlikely to be restored for quite a while as the roads are impassable. What am I grumbling about?

We are invited to Chris and Ann's for Christmas Day; they are great fun and we are looking forward to it. We shall have to take the dogs with us because we shall be away too long to leave them at home; they might wreck the place just out of boredom! Unfortunately Ann is allergic to dog fur, but we are going to put an old duvet in the back of the car and they will have to stay there most of the time. Christmas Day dawned bright and frosty, but no snow, so the roads were alright. We had not been to see the Chris and Ann since they moved to another house in the same village and we loved their new one. Ann's decorations were superb; she had made huge garlands which adorned the banisters and hall; every table and shelf had an arrangement, and under the tree was a small mountain of gifts, all so beautifully wrapped that they were decorations in themselves.

The smell of roasting turkey that soon assailed our nostrils promised gastronomic treats to come; we were not disappointed! Anne had cooked three kinds of stuffing, as well as all the other traditional accompaniments. By the time we had demolished all the goodies we were really in need of a walk (or a sleep!). We all donned woolly hats, boots etc. and then rescued the dogs from the car. After three hours cooped up, they were wildly excited and we could barely hold them. It was a superb day, the blue sky as clear as crystal and the sun, already almost on the horizon, was turning the world to gold. The frost nipped our noses and our breath hung in the air. The dogs pulled us joyfully along, with their noses in the grass verge inhaling all the exciting country smells. After the 'Sheep in the pond' experience of two Christmases ago, we kept them on their leads! Max was there too of course, but he ran free as an obedient well trained dog deserves to do. We walked for nearly an hour, watching the sun turn blood red and slowly sink out of sight; there was just a glow in the sky left to light us home. The temperature had plummeted by then and the cars had white hoar frost overcoats; there was no way we could put the dogs back in the car unless we left for home immediately as they would be frozen! Ann said we could bring them in and she would try to stay as far away from them as possible. Inside the house the warmth wrapped round us, thawing our frozen faces; beautiful as the countryside had been, we were glad to be back in the central heating!

Hardly had we got through the door, when the dogs surprised the elderly resident cat - who was not impressed by two huge cheeky strangers clamping their noses to her bum, and she fled upstairs to find refuge. We grabbed them just in time to prevent them following her. Their first black mark! Once inside any strange house they attempt to explore every inch; this is done at breakneck speed making as much noise as a herd of buffalo, hoovering up anything edible in passing, cat saucers being top favourite. We foiled this exercise by shutting the lounge door firmly and forcing them to lie at our feet. This they did for thirty seconds at a time before being reminded again - and again - and again. Max watched this with a superior expression. We were ashamed of them. They are no better behaved now than they were at six months old. They are completely unsquashable; it is so humiliating when Max does everything that Robert tells him.

Relative calm prevailed eventually and the presents were distributed and opened. Happy noises like "Oh super! "and "Smashing, how did you know that I wanted that!" accompanied the

Giblets for everyone. Cats have such lovely manners.

sound of tearing wrapping paper. All was well until the cat decided, dogs or no dogs, she wanted to join in. Ann let her in and Tom pounced on her, frightening her and us! Mercifully he did not hurt her, but it was not a friendly move and we were mortified. Rachael took her back to the bedroom and cuddled her until she relaxed. Tom got a stinging smack from David and Gill lay watching and looking smug, pretending that the thought of cat chasing had never entered his head. This episode spoilt the end of the day for me and they would have gone back into the car regardless of the sub-zero temperature, but when we tried to open it we found all the door locks were frozen solid. As we had then got them outside we walked them briskly down the road and back, while Robert and Chris worked on the doors with hot towels and anti-freeze and eventually got them open. Even the rubber seals had been frozen as well as the locks! Once we had scraped all the windows and got the engine running we still had to wait until it was warm enough to stop our breath freezing instantly on the wind screen, it was incredible! I drove home with my heart in my mouth along the ice coated country lanes. The stars were brilliant and we remembered the last time we had seen the sky like this down in Cornwall. It was much warmer on that occasion! The journey home was safely achieved and we fell into bed with the blissful thought that ahead lay seven potential lie-ins before work recalls us next week.

Our own Christmas party has now been and gone, with only the turkey bones left to show for it. The weather is still arctic but the blue skies have been replaced with freezing fog; and every leaf and twig is painted with spikes of ice. Walks have been wonderfully clean, the dogs have tried in vain to dig, but as the mud is as solid as our new concrete compost bins, they have not got very far! We have delayed cutting them because of the extreme cold and they look rather like black bears, very cuddly. I wonder how long it will be before a warmer spell gives us a chance to attend to their barbering - they are going to miss their lovely warm coats when the time comes!

Another page turned, another year begun, it is time to pause and reflect on these last four years. The dogs have changed and enriched our lives beyond our wildest imaginings. They have filled our days with love, laughter and fun, not to mention a seasoning of rage, and we expect they will continue alternately to entertain and annoy us with their antics for years to come. Gill has just appeared with David's wellington boot; he is carrying it with his nose inside, and as his eyes are inside too he has no idea where he is going! They are the clowns of the dog world. Our friends expressed doubts about our sanity when we took them on, but we know that it was the best thing we ever did, since our human family spread their wings and flew away.

Just in case you are tempted to follow in our mostly muddy footsteps, I have made a few notes to save you from yourself!

STANDARD POODLE - SPECIFICATIONS

1 Intelligent (thinks of it before you do.)

2 Lively personality (impossible to tire, still raring to go when you are knackered.)

3 Healthy (Vets bills a-plenty for cut paws, scratched eyes etc., but not for diseases.)

4 Gun dog (if he scents a rabbit you can say goodbye to him until he has caught it - and eaten it.)

5 Affectionate (knocks you down to kiss you, and brings you all of your garments and shoes, dribbled on or chewed, when you have been out for more than ten minutes.)

6 Good guard dog (wakes you at 2am. because the wind is swaying the trees.)

7 Criminal tendencies (is an incorrigible thief - nothing edible is safe, Tom even ate my lipstick!)

8 Their coats do not shed (they need cutting once every six weeks at vast expense and inconvienience.)

If you are still keen to own a standard Poodle - good luck, you will need it!

EXPLORING HISTORY ALL AROUND

by

Vivienne Evans

A handbook of local history, arranged as a series of routes to cover Bedfordshire and adjoining parts of Hertfordshire and Buckinghamshire. It is organised as two books in one. There are seven thematic sections full of fascinating historical detail and anecdotes for armchair reading. Also it is a perfect source of family days out as the book is organised as circular motoring/cycling explorations, highlighting attractions and landmarks.

Also included is a background history to all the major towns in the area, plus dozens of villages, which will enhance your appreciation and understanding of the history that is all around you!

A Book Castle Publication

CHILTERN WALKS
Hertfordshire, Bedfordshire and North Buckinghamshire
by
Nick Moon

This book is one of a series of three to provide a comprehensive coverage of walks throughout the whole of the Chiltern area (as defined by the Chiltern Society). The walks included vary in length from 3.0 to 10.9 miles, but are mainly in the 5-7 mile range popular for half-day walks, although suggestions of possible combinations of walks are given for those preferring a full day's walk.

Each walk gives details of nearby places of interest and is accompanied by a specially drawn map of the route which also indicates local pubs and a skeleton road network.

A Book Castle Publication

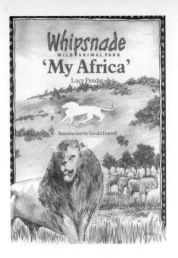

WHIPSNADE MY AFRICA
by
Lucy Pendar

The inside story of sixty years of this world-renowned institution, written from the unique viewpoint of a young girl living and growing up in Sir Peter Chalmers Mitchell's dream of an open-plan Zoo Park, the first of its kind in this country. Her father was the Resident Engineer who took her to Whipsnade Park just before it opened, thus leading her into an enchanted childhood.

As well as tracing the Park's full history, the book is full of anecdotes, both humorous and tragic, about its animals and people - all of whom she has known down the years. Despite eventually moving away in adult life, her enduring love affair with the place has never faltered. She has felt compelled to return again and again to follow its changing fortunes. With over 130 fascinating rare photographs and original line drawings, the book also contains an introduction by Gerald Durrell.

A Book Castle Publication

ELEPHANTS I'LL NEVER FORGET
A Keeper's Life at Whipsnade and London Zoo
by
John Weatherhead

Cheeky persistence earned an animal-mad teenager a coveted job at London Zoo and opened the door to years of amazing encounters with all manner of creatures from around the world.

After a decade there with birds and various mammals, he applied for a posting at Whipsnade, and by 28 he was Head Keeper of elephants. This story of elephants in captivity recounts the problems, the excitement and many amusing and tragic incidents, both behind the scenes and in the full public gaze.

But John's lifetime of experience with these massive creatures also involved instructive trips overseas - to Africa on Safari; for the establishment of a new zoo in Quatar; to transport elephants from Burma to Europe, and to ship a bull elephant from Switzerland to Japan in a passenger 'Jumbo'!

A Book Castle Publication